100 AMAZING FACTS ABOUT RUGBY

2024, Marc Dresgui

Index

Introduction 6
Fact 1 - Rugby was born of daring cheating.............................. 7
Fact 2 - The Six Nations Tournament: a European tradition................ 8
Fact 3 - Rugby XIII: a dynamic variant 9
Fact 4 - Rugby Sevens: the art of speed 10
Fact 5 - Scrimmages: collective strength and strategy.................. 11
Fact 6 - Keys: the game's aerial relaunches 12
Fact 7 - Transformations: crucial additional points 13
Fact 8 - Penalties: penalties and opportunities........................ 14
Fact 9 - Red and yellow cards: discipline on the pitch 15
Fact 10 - An oval ball for a unique game 17
Fact 11 - Player positions: specific roles 18
Fact 12 - Rugby's iconic captains...................................... 19
Fact 13 - Points records in international matches 20
Fact 14 - Rugby's greatest rivalries................................... 21
Fact 15 - British and Irish Lions tours................................ 22
Fact 16 - The Rugby World Cup: a global event 23
Fact 17 - The invincible teams: a series of historic victories 24
Fact 18 - Versatile players: mastering several positions 25
Fact 19 - National anthems: emotional pre-match moments 26
Fact 20 - The All Blacks and their intimidating haka 28
Fact 21 - Team mascots: symbols and good luck charms 29
Fact 22 - National team nicknames...................................... 30
Fact 23 - Centenary clubs: history and tradition 31
Fact 24 - Local derbies: high-voltage matches 32
Fact 25 - Summer touring: international challenges..................... 33
Fact 26 - The evolving rules of rugby 34
Fact 27 - Equipment: from leather to synthetics 35
Fact 28 - Cleats: grip and performance 36
Fact 29 - The jerseys: iconic colors and designs 37
Fact 30 - Referees: guarantors of the rules of the game............... 39
Fact 31 - Rugby balls: evolution and manufacture...................... 40
Fact 32 - Club anthems: fan songs 41
Fact 33 - Barbarians tours: spirit of the game........................ 42
Fact 34 - Record stadium crowds 43
Fact 35 - The longest rugby matches ever played 44
Fact 36 - The biggest comebacks 45
Fact 37 - The most capped players in history 46
Fact 38 - The youngest and oldest international players................ 47
Fact 39 - Rugby families: sporting dynasties 48
Fact 40 - Players scoring after a delayed whistle 50
Fact 41 - Amateur players turned professionals........................ 51
Fact 42 - The most expensive transfers in rugby 52
Fact 43 - Famous injuries and triumphant returns...................... 53

Fact 44 - Players who have successfully changed sport..........................54
Fact 45 - Legendary coaches and their philosophies 55
Fact 46 - Women's teams: growth and success.....................................56
Fact 47 - The smallest players in history 57
Fact 48 - The fastest match tries...58
Fact 49 - The longest international careers..59
Fact 50 - The drop goal: a decisive kick..61
Fact 51 - Players who have scored in more than one World Cup...........62
Fact 52 - Grand Slam winning teams..63
Fact 53 - Matches played with historical equipment............................64
Fact 54 - Teams with midnight matches 65
Fact 55 - Matches played on unusual pitches 66
Fact 56 - Teams who played with underdogs...67
Fact 57 - Matches decided by kicks after extra time 68
Fact 58 - Players who have played for two different nations 69
Fact 59 - Teams with back-to-back titles...70
Fact 60 - Tackling: technique and safety in action................................72
Fact 61 - Largest point spreads in the finals...73
Fact 62 - Matches with the most tries...74
Fact 63 - Players who have scored all their team's points.....................75
Fact 64 - Teams having won all their matches on a tour 76
Fact 65 - Longest interrupted losing streaks...77
Fact 66 - Players who have played in several professional leagues........78
Fact 67 - Teams that have won titles in more than one country.............79
Fact 68 - Closed-door matches: reasons and impact 80
Fact 69 - Teams with memorable charity matches.................................81
Fact 70 - Speed records in the field 83
Fact 71 - Players who inspire fictional characters 84
Fact 72 - Players who broke longevity records 85
Fact 73 - Teams having played matches on several continents..............86
Fact 74 - Players who scored after intercepting passes........................87
Fact 75 - Players voted best player more than once..............................88
Fact 76 - Players who have been coaches at the same time 89
Fact 77 - Players who scored with unexpected combinations...............90
Fact 78 - Teams who have won major tournaments as underdogs 91
Fact 79 - Players who were captains at a young age 92
Fact 80 - Rugby's biggest stars...94
Fact 81 - Players selected after a position change................................95
Fact 82 - Matches played with customized balls....................................96
Fact 83 - Matches played on unusual artificial pitches..........................97
Fact 84 - Teams playing with fans in disguise 98
Fact 85 - Players selected in two different sports 99
Fact 86 - Teams that have used unprecedented defensive formations 100
Fact 87 - Matches played with guest referees 101
Fact 88 - Players who scored with unforeseen kicks 102
Fact 89 - Teams with record consecutive wins....................................103
Fact 90 - Trials: key moments of the match 105

Fact 91 - Matches played to celebrate historic anniversaries 106
Fact 92 - Matches played with mixed gender teams 107
Fact 93 - Players selected for unexpected moves................................ 108
Fact 94 - Games played to attract new spectators 109
Fact 95 - Players who scored after defensive errors............................ 110
Fact 96 - Matches played with giant rugby balls.................................. 111
Fact 97 - Matches played to promote sporting values 112
Fact 98 - Games played with futuristic equipment 113
Fact 99 - Teams who played matches at extreme altitudes................. 114
Fact 100 - World rugby's legendary stadiums...................................... 116
Conclusion 117
Quiz.. 118
Answers 122

"Rugby is a hooligan's game played by gentlemen."

- Winston Churchill

Introduction

Welcome to the exciting world of rugby! You're about to dive into a book filled with incredible stories, impressive records and unforgettable moments. Rugby is much more than just a sport: it's a blend of strength, strategy and team spirit. Whether you're already a big fan or just want to discover this unique game, this book has been written for you, with amazing Facts that will take you on a journey through history, across the world's pitches, and even behind the scenes of the biggest matches.

You might be wondering why rugby is so special? It's a sport with fascinating rules, courageous players and moments when everything can change in a second. It's also a sport where respect for others is an essential value, whether it's for your teammates, your opponents or even the referee. Here, everyone has an important role to play, whether you're small or big, fast or powerful. You'll discover anecdotes about legendary players, incredible stadiums and matches that have made history.

Each Fact in this book reveals a different facet of this extraordinary sport. You'll learn how an oval ball can create unpredictable bounces, how a scrum works like a giant jigsaw puzzle, or why certain moves, like the drop goal, require incredible precision. Some Facts will make you smile, others will surprise you, and maybe some will make you want to try rugby yourself!

Rugby is also a human adventure. Behind every match, there are players who train hard, fans who thrill to every action, and teams who show that together, we can achieve great things. This book will show you how rugby has spanned the ages and continents, and how it continues to unite millions of people around the same values: courage, solidarity and respect.

So, are you ready to take to the field? Strap on your cleats (or rather, open this book wide!) and get ready to discover 100 Amazing Facts about rugby. Whether you're curious, passionate or just a dreamer, there's a story here for you. Come on, let's go on an oval adventure you won't soon forget!

Marc Dresqui

Fact 1 - Rugby was born of daring cheating

Once upon a time, in England, there lived a young boy named William Webb Ellis. He was at school in Rugby, a small town in England, in 1823. One day, during a soccer match (a very popular sport in those days), William did something incredible. While everyone was playing by the rules, he suddenly grabbed the ball in his hands and ran towards the opposing team's goal. A totally forbidden gesture!

This unexpected moment provoked a mixture of amazement and excitement among the other students. Back then, soccer rules were much more flexible than they are today. Onlookers wondered: why not invent a game based on this idea? This event gave birth to a new sport, in which running while holding the ball became not only permitted, but essential. The sport was named rugby, in homage to the school where it all began.

Of course, this anecdote has survived the years, but some historians doubt its veracity. Nevertheless, it remains the most widely-told legend about the birth of rugby. What is certain is that the Rugby School played a central role in establishing the first rules of the sport, known as the "Rugby Rules", laying the foundations for this unique game.

In its early days, rugby was more of a rough and tumble game than the sport we know today. There were no referees or precise rules, and players often found themselves in veritable scrum to wrestle the ball away from each other. Gradually, the pupils of the Rugby School began to structure the game, adding rules to govern physical contact and define ways of scoring points.

The sport, which became popular with Rugby students, soon spread to other English schools and universities. Each school added its own rules, making matches often confusing. In 1871, a group of amateurs decided to standardize these rules by creating the Rugby Football Union (RFU). This organization gave rugby a clear identity and official rules.

Today, rugby is played all over the world and has come a long way since William Webb Ellis decided to defy the rules. But this story of daring cheating reminds us that sometimes, daring something new can change the course of history. Rugby continues to rally millions of players and fans around this simple idea: run, pass, score... and above all, excel.

Fact 2 - The Six Nations Tournament: a European tradition

Every year in Europe, a major rugby tournament brings together six of the continent's best national teams: England, France, Ireland, Italy, Scotland and Wales. The tournament is one of the world's oldest sporting events, first held in 1883 under the name of Home Nations Championship, pitting only England, Scotland, Ireland and Wales against each other.

France joined the tournament in 1910, transforming it into the Five Nations. This change made the matches even more exciting, as France brought a different style of play, often faster and more creative. It wasn't until 2000 that Italy was added, giving birth to the Six Nations Tournament we know today. Since then, the Italians have been striving to compete with their neighbors.

The tournament takes place every year between February and March. During this period, teams compete in a unique format where each nation plays all the others once. The team that finishes with the most victories takes the trophy. If a team beats all the others, it achieves what is known as a "Grand Slam", a rare and prestigious feat.

Each match is played in one of Europe's most famous stadiums, such as the Stade de France in Paris or Twickenham in London. These historic venues vibrate with an incredible atmosphere, where the chants of the fans and the colorful flags make each match unforgettable. Matches between rival nations, such as England versus Scotland, are particularly intense and passionately followed.

The Six Nations Tournament is not just about rugby. It's also a time of celebration for fans. The towns hosting the matches become festive places, where rugby fans from all over the world come together to share their love of the sport. The tournament is a symbol of unity and friendly competition between close, but often rival, countries.

Over its 140-year history, the tournament has become much more than just a sporting competition. It embodies the values of rugby: respect, team spirit and surpassing oneself. The Six Nations is an unmissable event that reminds us every year why this sport is so special.

Fact 3 - Rugby XIII: a dynamic variant

XIII rugby is an exciting, fast-paced version of rugby that originated in England in 1895. At the time, a dispute broke out between clubs in the north and south of the country over financial compensation for players. The northern clubs decided to split up and create their own discipline, more suited to working-class people. This was the birth of XIII rugby.

This variant is distinguished by its high tempo and simplified rules. Unlike XV rugby, each team has thirteen players, leaving more space on the pitch. Matches are played in two forty-minute periods, and contact is strictly controlled. After six attempts to advance, the team must give the ball back to the opponent, making the game even more strategic.

One of the big differences in XIII rugby is the way it scores. Players try to score tries, just like in XV rugby, but the point values are different. A try is worth four points, and a successful conversion is worth two more. Penalties and drops are also worth fewer points, encouraging teams to play offensively and take risks.

This variant is particularly popular in Australia, New Zealand and certain regions of France, notably Occitanie. French clubs such as XIII Catalan and Dragons Catalans have left their mark on the history of the sport. In Australia, the National Rugby League (NRL) attracts millions of spectators, featuring outstanding players such as Andrew Johns, a legend of the sport.

Rugby à XIII is also known for its inclusiveness and diversity. It is played by men, women and youngsters in numerous competitions. What's more, it has paved the way for adapted versions, such as armchair rugby, to enable people with disabilities to play this intense, tactical sport.

This sport, often overshadowed by rugby union, shines for its speed and accessibility. Fans appreciate the spectacle offered by its fast-paced action and turnarounds. With its unique style and strong values, XIII rugby is a perfect example of the richness and diversity that rugby can offer.

Fact 4 - Rugby Sevens: the art of speed

Rugby Sevens is an intense, fast-paced version of rugby, with each team fielding just seven players instead of fifteen. Originating in Scotland in 1883, this format was created to make matches shorter and more accessible to more teams. Today, the sport is known for its frenetic pace, spectacular action and incredibly fast players.

The rules of rugby à VII are similar to those of rugby à XV, but matches last just 14 minutes, divided into two halves of seven minutes each. With fewer players on the field, space is greater, forcing teams to run more. As a result, tries are frequent, and every defensive error can turn into a point.

This format emphasizes specific qualities: speed, agility and precision. Players must not only run very fast, but also make instant decisions. The ball moves quickly through the hands, and long passes are common. This style of play attracts many spectators thanks to its spectacular and dynamic nature.

Rugby Sevens is particularly popular at the World Rugby Sevens Series, a tournament held in several countries each year. Teams from Fiji, New Zealand and South Africa often dominate the competition, thanks to legendary players such as Waisale Serevi, nicknamed the "King of Rugby Sevens". His dazzling runs and precise passes have left their mark on the history of the sport.

Rugby Sevens also has an important international dimension. In 2016, it entered the Olympic Games, a historic milestone for the sport. This success shows just how much it is appreciated around the world. The Olympic matches offered an incredible spectacle, with fast-paced action and memorable turnarounds.

This unique format offers a different experience to classic rugby. It showcases exceptionally talented players and demonstrates just how varied the sport can be. With its breathless pace and intense encounters, rugby sevens is a true tribute to the art of speed and agility.

Fact 5 - Scrimmages: collective strength and strategy

The scrum is one of rugby's most impressive actions. It occurs when play is interrupted due to a minor foul, such as a forwards foul. At this point, the eight forwards from each team form a compact formation to link up and try to push their opponents backwards. It's an incredible display of strength and coordination.

The scrum begins with a gesture called the "introduction", in which the scrum-half slides the ball between the two teams. The front-row players, called heelers, then try to recover the ball with their feet, while the other forwards push with all their might. Scrummaging requires both physical strength and excellent technique to maintain balance and avoid penalties.

It's also a moment of strategy, when each team tries to gain the upper hand. Players communicate with each other by signaling or shouting to coordinate their efforts. A good scrum can give a team a favorable position to launch a quick attack or even score a try. In some matches, scrum superiority makes all the difference.

Scrummaging requires rigorous preparation. The forwards train to synchronize their movements and build up their stamina. It's a collective effort in which every player counts. If just one player breaks away or pushes too early, the scrum can collapse, resulting in a penalty for his team. That's why discipline and concentration are essential at this key moment in the game.

Some scrummages have gone down in rugby history. For example, during the 2011 Six Nations Tournament, Wales' scrum against Ireland was so powerful that it completely reversed the course of the match. These spectacular moments remain engraved in the memories of fans and demonstrate the importance of this phase of the game.

The scrum symbolizes the very essence of rugby: collective strength, total commitment and the will to triumph together. Every scrum is a battle in which team spirit and strategy often win out over sheer physical strength. It's a fascinating moment for players and spectators alike.

Fact 6 - Keys: the game's aerial relaunches

The touchline is one of rugby's most spectacular moments. It occurs when a player kicks the ball out of bounds. To resume play, a throw-in is taken. The forwards of both teams gather in parallel lines, ready to leap forward to catch the ball thrown from the edge of the field by the hooker.

The throw-in is a precise technical gesture. The hooker must throw the ball straight and into the designated area, while avoiding the opponents' hands. To optimize their chances of recovering the ball, the players on the lined-up team use secret calls and strategies. These signals determine who will jump and in which direction the ball will be thrown.

During a touchdown, jumpers are often the tallest and most powerful players on the team. To maximize their height, they are lifted by two teammates called lifters. It's an impressive moment: these athletes rise into the air, arms outstretched, in an attempt to grab the ball. The team that recovers the ball can then quickly restart play.

The touch requires perfect coordination between the players. If the throw is too short or too long, or if the lifters miss their timing, the ball risks being recovered by the opposing team. Sometimes, touches become real aerial battles, with both teams vying for the upper hand. These duels are often decisive for the outcome of the match.

Some key touches remain etched in rugby history. At the 1995 World Cup, South Africa used their dominance of the touchline to control their matches and win the title. This strategy demonstrated the importance of mastering this phase of the game. A well-executed touch can even lead to a try moments later.

The touch is much more than a simple restart of the game. It's a blend of strength, precision and tactics that highlights the team's collective spirit. At each restart, players and spectators alike hold their breath, fascinated by this aerial dance unique to rugby.

Fact 7 - Transformations: crucial additional points

When a team scores a try in rugby, they have the opportunity to transform this success by scoring additional points. This moment, known as the "transformation", involves kicking the ball between the posts and over the crossbar. It's a delicate exercise that can make the difference in a tight match.

The conversion is attempted from a point aligned with the spot where the try was scored. If the try is scored close to the touchline, kicking becomes very difficult. That's why players often try to score their tries as close to the posts as possible. This makes the conversion easier and increases the chances of success.

The player designated to carry out the transformation is often a kicking specialist. These players train for hours to master their precision and power. They use precise technique, placing the ball on a tee, taking off with concentration and carefully calculating their trajectory. The slightest mistake can cost them precious points.

Some transformations have left their mark on the history of rugby. In 2003, during the World Cup final, Jonny Wilkinson pulled off an essential conversion for England, showing just how crucial this technical gesture is. Each successful conversion gives the team two extra points, which can turn a draw into victory.

The moment of transformation is often full of suspense for the spectators. The stadium falls silent as the goalscorer prepares, each fan holding his or her breath. Then, as the ball passes between the posts, there is an explosion of joy or a sigh of disappointment, depending on the team being supported.

Transformations symbolize the importance of precision and technical mastery in rugby. They add a strategic dimension to the game, because every point counts. These kicks show that, even in a contact sport, finesse and concentration play an essential role.

Fact 8 - Penalties: penalties and opportunities

In rugby, a penalty is awarded when a team commits a serious offence, such as offside or a dangerous tackle. The opposing team is then awarded a penalty kick, a valuable opportunity to score points or advance down the field. It can also be a strategic opportunity to regain control of the match.

If the team chooses to attempt a kick to score points, the ball must pass between the posts and over the crossbar. A successful penalty earns three points, making it an attractive option, especially in tight games. The player designated to take the penalty must demonstrate precision and composure, because every point counts.

Penalties aren't just for scoring points. Another option is to kick for touch, allowing the team to gain ground and regain possession of the ball through a touch. This strategy is often used when a team is far from the opposing posts and wants to get closer to launch an attack.

A third possibility is to play the penalty quickly by lightly tapping the ball and running with it. This bold choice, often made by fast, creative players, can surprise the opposing team. It creates unexpected opportunities to make rapid progress and put the defense to the sword.

Some penalties have gone down in rugby history. In 1995, during the World Cup, Joel Stransky, a South African player, scored decisive penalties for his team. These precise kicks helped South Africa win their first world title. This example shows how penalties can change the course of a match.

Penalties embody the balance between sanction and opportunity. They are a reminder of the importance of respecting the rules, while offering teams the chance to demonstrate their strategy and technical mastery. This intense moment is often decisive, adding a touch of suspense and tactics to rugby.

Fact 9 - Red and yellow cards: discipline on the pitch

Red and yellow cards are essential tools for maintaining discipline on the rugby pitch. They enable the referee to penalize behavior that endangers players or goes against the rules of the game. These cards are a reminder of the importance of respect in a sport where physical contact is constant.

The yellow card is used to temporarily exclude a player. When a player commits a serious foul, such as a dangerous tackle or intentional obstruction, the referee may show him a yellow card. This means the player must leave the field for ten minutes. This sanction can weaken the team, as it finds itself outnumbered.

The red card, on the other hand, is a definitive expulsion. It is reserved for extremely serious offences, such as deliberate violence or unsportsmanlike behaviour. When a player receives a red card, he or she may not return to the pitch, and the team must play the rest of the match with one player less. This sanction often has a huge impact on the outcome of a match.

Cards are also a way for referees to protect players. Rugby is a sport of intense contact, and the rules are designed to ensure everyone's safety. For example, high tackles that hit the head or neck are strictly forbidden. By using cards, the referee sends a clear message: safety comes first.

A famous example of the use of cards occurred at the 2019 World Cup. In a match between England and Argentina, an Argentine player was shown the red card for a dangerous tackle. This decision, although contested by some fans, was praised for its firmness and respect for safety rules.

Red and yellow cards are not just sanctions. They teach players and spectators alike the importance of respecting rules and opponents. These often dramatic moments are a reminder that rugby, for all its intensity, remains a sport where respect and discipline are paramount.

Fact 10 - An oval ball for a unique game

Rugby stands out from many other sports thanks to its oval ball, an emblematic element that makes the game so special. Unlike the round balls used in sports such as soccer, the rugby ball has an elongated shape. This unique feature is not just aesthetic: it profoundly influences the way the game is played, adding strategic challenges and opportunities.

Originally, the first rugby balls were made from pigs' bladders, inflated at the mouth and then covered with leather. Their oval shape was due to the natural shape of these bladders, not to a deliberate choice. The balls were all different, some rounder, others more elongated, adding a dose of unpredictability to the game.

Over time, the oval shape was standardized, as it offered specific advantages. It makes it easier to hold the ball in the hands when running or tackling. What's more, when thrown or kicked, the oval ball produces unpredictable trajectories, making the game even more exciting. Bounces are also irregular, forcing players to keep their wits about them at all times.

Today's rugby balls are made of synthetic materials to withstand the elements. Their rough surface guarantees a better grip, even in the rain. They measure around 28 centimetres in length and weigh between 410 and 460 grams. These dimensions are carefully respected to ensure fairness in matches and maintain uniformity in competitions.

A famous rugby ball moment occurred during a match between England and Australia in 2003. Jonny Wilkinson, the English striker, used the shape of the ball to make a perfect drop goal, giving his team victory. This feat illustrates the importance of understanding and mastering this very special ball.

The oval ball is more than just a tool: it embodies the very essence of rugby. Its unique shape has not only shaped the game, but also symbolizes the spirit of innovation that marked the birth of the sport. Players and spectators alike know that every pass, every kick and every rebound tells a story that only an oval ball can.

Fact 11 - Player positions: specific roles

In rugby, each player occupies a well-defined position with a precise role, adapted to his or her strengths and skills. The team is made up of fifteen players, divided between forwards and backs. This organization enables all phases of the game to be covered, from scrummaging to touchdowns and fast attacks. Each position has its own importance and contributes to the team's success.

The eight forwards are the "engines" of the team. Powerful and robust, they are responsible for scrummaging and rucks, where physical strength is essential. Among them, the hooker is responsible for throw-ins and plays a key role in scrummaging. The second and third lines provide support and dynamism, covering a large part of the field.

The backs, of which there are seven, rely more on speed and strategy. The scrum-half is an agile player who passes the ball quickly after a scrum or ruck. The fly-half, often considered the brain of the team, makes crucial decisions by directing play with precise passes or kicks.

As for the centers, they form a complementary duo. The first center is often a solid player who breaks through the opponent's defense, while the second center is faster and tasked with outflanking opponents. Finally, wingers and full-backs complete the back line. Wingers, positioned on the flanks, are real sprinters, while the full-back is the last line of defence and an excellent returner.

A famous example of a versatile player is Jonny Wilkinson, England's legendary fly-half. Thanks to his vision and precise kicking, he led his team to victory in the 2003 World Cup. This example shows how one position can make the difference in a decisive match.

Each position is unique, but no player can succeed alone. Rugby is a team sport where coordination and solidarity are paramount. Every player, whether forward or back-rower, knows that his or her role is crucial in moving the ball forward and scoring points. It's this diversity of skills that makes the sport so fascinating.

Fact 12 - Rugby's iconic captains

In rugby, the captain plays an essential role. More than just a player, he guides his team on the field and makes important decisions during the match, such as whether to take a penalty or kick for touch. The best captains are often natural leaders, respected by their team-mates for their charisma, vision and determination.

One of the most famous captains is Richie McCaw, who led the New Zealand team, the All Blacks, to back-to-back World Cup victories in 2011 and 2015. McCaw was known for his game intelligence and ability to inspire his teammates. Under his leadership, the All Blacks made history by becoming one of the most feared teams in the world.

Another iconic captain is Martin Johnson, who led England to victory at the 2003 World Cup. Johnson, an imposing second row, was a true leader on the pitch. His ability to motivate his team and remain calm under pressure was crucial at decisive moments, notably during the final against Australia, won thanks to a legendary drop goal.

Women's rugby also has its emblematic figures, such as Fiao'o Fa'amausili, former captain of New Zealand's Black Ferns. Under her leadership, the Black Ferns won several World Cups. Fa'amausili was admired for her commitment and influence on the game, becoming an inspiration to many young players around the world.

Captains don't just lead their teams on the pitch. They are also role models off the pitch, representing their team and country with pride. During national anthems, it's often the captain who the cameras focus on, as he embodies the hope and determination of his team.

Every rugby team needs a captain to coordinate its efforts and embody its values. These exemplary players show that leadership is measured not only by physical strength, but also by the ability to inspire, unite and face challenges with courage and intelligence.

Fact 13 - Points records in international matches

Rugby is a sport where scoring points is essential to victory. In some international matches, outstanding players have set impressive records, scoring an incredible number of points in a single match. These feats testify not only to their talent, but also to the collective strength of their team.

One of the most famous records belongs to Simon Culhane, a New Zealand player. In 1995, during a World Cup match between New Zealand and Japan, he scored 45 points alone. Thanks to his tries, conversions and penalties, he helped the All Blacks to a crushing victory, scoring 145 points that day. This record remains unsurpassed.

Another remarkable feat was achieved by Scottish legend Gavin Hastings. Also in 1995, against Côte d'Ivoire, Hastings scored 44 points. His ability to turn almost any opportunity into a point left a lasting impression. This record shows the importance of precision and composure in decisive moments.

International matches between great teams also offer spectacular records. In 2007, Jonny Wilkinson, England's famous fly-half, shone in several matches, becoming one of the highest points scorers in World Cup history. His precise kicking often turned games in England's favor.

Scoring records aren't limited to men. In women's rugby, Portia Woodman, a New Zealand player, scored an impressive number of tries at the 2017 World Cup, demonstrating the importance of female try scorers in the evolution of international rugby.

These records show that rugby is a sport where individual technique and teamwork intertwine to produce incredible feats. Players who reach such heights leave their mark on the history of the sport, inspiring future generations.

Fact 14 - Rugby's greatest rivalries

Rugby is a sport where rivalries between national or club teams can become epic. These confrontations, often marked by a long history, captivate fans and give rise to unforgettable matches. These rivalries are not only sporting, but also reflect cultures, traditions and a deep mutual respect.

One of the most famous rivalries is that between England and France, often referred to as the "Crunch". These two teams face off every year in the Six Nations Tournament. This duel is more than just a match: it's a clash between two different styles of play, one structured and powerful, the other creative and unpredictable. These encounters are often hotly contested.

In Oceania, the rivalry between New Zealand and Australia is one of the oldest and most intense. These two nations have dominated rugby for decades. Their clashes, particularly in the Rugby Championship, are renowned for their physical intensity and exceptional technical level. The All Blacks and Wallabies don't just play: they fight for supremacy in their region.

Another rugby classic is the duel between Ireland and Wales. These two nations, who share a rich and complex history, compete every year in the Six Nations Tournament. Their matches are often marked by an electric atmosphere, with fans singing at the top of their lungs, making each encounter memorable.

In the southern hemisphere, the rivalry between South Africa and New Zealand is also legendary. These two teams have often played in World Cup finals, such as the one in 1995, when Nelson Mandela presented the trophy to the Springboks. These matches embody the values of rugby: respect, courage and surpassing oneself.

These great rivalries have shaped the history of rugby, giving players the opportunity to give their all. For the fans, they are an opportunity to thrill and celebrate their passion for the sport. Each emotionally-charged match is a reminder that rugby, beyond the scores, is a bond between nations.

Fact 15 - British and Irish Lions tours

The British and Irish Lions are a unique rugby team. Made up of the best players from England, Scotland, Wales and Ireland, this squad comes together every four years for memorable international tours. These sporting journeys, which date back to the late XIXe century, offer exciting duels against the best teams in the southern hemisphere.

The first Lions tours were organized in 1888. Back then, the team traveled by boat, playing dozens of matches against local teams in Australia and New Zealand. These tours were also a human adventure, where players discovered new cultures while sharing their passion for rugby. The matches, often played in difficult conditions, were marked by an impressive physical intensity.

Over the years, Lions tours have focused on a series of test matches against the great nations of the southern hemisphere: South Africa, New Zealand and Australia. Each tour includes three test matches, in which the Lions face the national team of the host country. These matches are moments of rare intensity, when rugby reaches its highest level.

In 1974, during a tour of South Africa, the Lions won a historic series. Under the leadership of captain Willie John McBride, they went 22 matches unbeaten, a feat never equalled. Their style of play, combining power and finesse, inspired a whole generation of players and left its mark on rugby history.

Lions tours are not just about matches. They are also an opportunity for players from different British and Irish nations to form a real team, sharing their strengths and overcoming their differences. The Lions team spirit is a model of cooperation and camaraderie, symbolizing the very best of rugby.

The British and Irish Lions represent a rare tradition in modern sport. These tours combine moments of intense rivalry with rich cultural exchanges, while honoring the values of rugby: respect, courage and the enjoyment of the game. For players and supporters alike, they are unforgettable events.

Fact 16 - The Rugby World Cup: a global event

The Rugby World Cup is one of the world's greatest sporting events. It brings together the best national teams every four years, in a competition where every match can be decisive. The tournament, which began in 1987, is now a global celebration of rugby, attracting millions of fans and television viewers.

The first edition took place in New Zealand and Australia. The All Blacks, as the New Zealand team was nicknamed, won the trophy by beating France in the final. This inaugural tournament showed the world the intensity and beauty of international rugby, laying the foundations for the event's continued success.

The trophy awarded to the winners is called the Webb Ellis Cup, in homage to William Webb Ellis, considered the inventor of rugby. The trophy symbolizes excellence and self-transcendence. Every player who touches it writes an important page in the history of the sport, whether in close matches or memorable exploits.

Some World Cup moments remain etched in the memory. In 1995, South Africa won the tournament on home soil, under the eyes of Nelson Mandela. This success went beyond sport, symbolizing the unity and reconciliation of a divided nation. The image of Mandela handing the trophy to Springbok captain François Pienaar has become a universal symbol of peace.

The World Cup is also a showcase for talented players. New Zealand star Jonah Lomu made his mark on the 1995 edition with his impressive runs and spectacular trials. His performances showed that this tournament is not just a competition, but also a place where legends are born.

This global event showcases the diversity of rugby, with teams from different continents such as Fiji, Japan and Argentina shining with their unique style. The World Cup is more than just a tournament: it's a celebration of rugby and its values of respect, courage and passion, bringing together players and fans from all over the world.

Fact 17 - The invincible teams: a series of historic victories

In the history of rugby, certain teams have left their mark on the game with impressive winning streaks. These "invincible" teams dominated their opponents thanks to their talent, strategy and collective spirit, becoming legends of the sport. Their exploits remain engraved in the memories of fans and inspire future generations.

New Zealand's All Blacks, known for their intimidating haka, are often cited as one of the most dominant teams in history. Between 2015 and 2016, they racked up 18 consecutive victories, beating teams from all over the world. Their tactical discipline and speed have made them a true winning machine, redefining the standards of international rugby.

South Africa, another great rugby nation, also enjoyed a memorable run. In 1995, after winning the World Cup, the Springboks went on a 17-game winning streak. Their powerful style of play, combined with an almost impenetrable defense, made them a feared team. This series remains a source of pride for South African fans.

In Europe, England made history between 2002 and 2003, culminating in their World Cup victory. Under the leadership of Martin Johnson and thanks to the precise kicking of Jonny Wilkinson, this team made rugby history. Their series included victories over formidable opponents such as Australia and New Zealand.

Invincible teams are not limited to rugby union. In rugby sevens, the Fijians are famous for their dominance. Their spectacular, fast-paced style of play has seen them win numerous tournaments without losing a single match. Their run at the 2016 World Rugby Sevens Series is particularly impressive.

These series of victories show that rugby is a sport where consistency and preparation count as much as individual talent. To be invincible, even temporarily, requires hard work, excellent team cohesion and an unshakeable will. These feats are a reminder of why rugby is a sport where the collective spirit always triumphs.

Fact 18 - Versatile players: mastering several positions

In rugby, each position has specific responsibilities, but some players possess a rare quality: versatility. These athletes, capable of playing in several positions, offer valuable flexibility to their teams. Being versatile requires not only varied skills, but also a thorough understanding of the game's strategies and dynamics.

A versatile player can change positions according to his team's needs. For example, New Zealand's Beauden Barrett excels at both full-back and fly-half. His speed and vision enable him to adapt quickly to these different roles, making the All Blacks unpredictable on the pitch.

Versatility is often called for when it comes to injuries or replacements. A player who can cover several positions can fill absences without compromising the balance of the team. Jonny Wilkinson, the famous fly-half, has also played as a center in certain situations, showing that his talent goes beyond his main role.

To be versatile, a player needs to master a variety of skills. A winger who becomes a full-back has to learn how to handle restarts and kicking under pressure. Similarly, a versatile forward may be called upon to play in the third or second row, requiring adjustments in technique and stamina.

Coaches particularly appreciate versatile players, as they allow them to create more varied strategies. Scott Barrett, Beauden's brother, is a case in point among the forwards. Capable of playing in both the second and third rows, he offers the All Blacks a strategic flexibility that complicates the task of their opponents.

Versatile players embody the very essence of rugby: adaptability, team spirit and hard work. By mastering multiple positions, they show that it's possible to go beyond expectations and contribute to the team in exceptional ways. These athletes inspire young players to diversify their skills to become indispensable assets.

Fact 19 - National anthems: emotional pre-match moments

National anthems are one of rugby's most moving moments. Before each international match, players from both teams gather to sing their national anthem, often surrounded by their supporters. These solemn moments mark the start of the battle, uniting players and fans in a single surge of pride and passion.

The anthem is much more than a song: it's a symbol of identity. For the players, singing it before a match is a way of showing their commitment to their country. Some, with tears in their eyes, are overwhelmed by emotion. These moments remind us that rugby is more than just a sport; it's a celebration of nations and cultures.

Anthems create a unique atmosphere in stadiums. Imagine a match between Ireland and Wales, where the Irish fans sing "Ireland's Call" while the Welsh sing "Hen Wlad Fy Nhadau". These songs, sung at the top of their lungs, resonate in the stands, transporting players and spectators alike into a moment of intense communion.

One of the most striking anthems is South Africa's "Nkosi Sikelel' iAfrika". This anthem, sung in several languages, symbolizes the unity of a once-divided country. During the 1995 World Cup final, the South African players sang this anthem with particular intensity, inspiring their supporters and leaving a lasting impression.

The audience also plays a crucial role in these moments. During the New Zealand anthem, "God Defend New Zealand", the All Blacks fans accompany the players in a way that thrills the whole stadium. These collective chants add an incredible energy, giving the matches an almost magical dimension.

National anthems are moments of pure emotion, when rugby becomes much more than a game. They demonstrate the attachment of players and supporters to their roots, while reminding us of the values of the sport: respect, pride and unity. These moments, intense and unforgettable, remain engraved in the memory of all those who experience them.

Fact 20 - The All Blacks and their intimidating haka

The All Blacks, New Zealand's rugby team, are famous for their haka, a Maori war dance performed before each match. This powerful and impressive ritual, which combines singing, gestures and piercing glances, is much more than a simple performance: it's a cultural tradition deeply rooted in the identity of the team and the country.

The All Blacks' best-known haka is called the "Ka Mate". Created in the XIXe century by a Maori chief, it celebrates victory and survival after battle. When the All Blacks perform it on the field, they honor their Maori ancestors while affirming their strength and determination in the face of their opponents.

The haka is a statement of intimidation. Imagine the players lined up in tight formation, their voices echoing around the stadium, their hands clapping their thighs in rhythm. Every movement is synchronized with impressive precision, and their facial expressions show intense concentration. For opponents, it's impossible not to feel a mixture of apprehension and admiration.

This ritual is also a moment of unity for the players. Even before the match begins, they come together and draw on their shared culture and history. The haka is a demonstration of their team spirit, showing that they play not only for themselves, but also for their country and its traditions.

Some memorable All Blacks matches have become famous for the haka. In 2007, during the World Cup, they performed a special haka, called "Kapa o Pango", before a match against France. This haka, even more intense than the Ka Mate, made a lasting impression with its power and novelty, making the moment unforgettable.

The All Blacks haka is much more than a sporting ritual. It's an expression of pride, strength and respect for their origins. This unique moment, which precedes every match, is a true signature of the team, showing the world that rugby can be much more than just a game.

Fact 21 - Team mascots: symbols and good luck charms

Mascots are emblematic characters that represent rugby teams. These figures, often amusing or impressive, are not just decorative: they embody the team's values and play an important role in bringing fans together. These symbols are both good luck charms and ambassadors of the rugby spirit, on and off the pitch.

Each mascot tells a story linked to the identity of the team it represents. For example, the mascot of the South African Springboks is a springbok, a fast and graceful animal that embodies the qualities of this formidable team. The All Blacks, although they have no official mascot, are often associated with the kiwi, an emblematic bird of New Zealand.

During matches, mascots play a key role in the entertainment. Dressed in colorful costumes, they parade around the pitch, cheering on the fans and adding to the festive atmosphere. They are particularly popular with children, who love to interact with them and take photos with them. These moments strengthen the bond between the team and its fans.

Some European clubs have famous mascots, such as Maximus le Coq, who represents the French national team. Maximus, with his blue suit and proud attitude, embodies the fighting spirit of Les Bleus. During the Six Nations Tournament, he motivates the French fans with his dances and acrobatics, adding a touch of humor to the matches.

Mascots are not confined to stadiums. They often take part in charity events, visit schools and appear in awareness campaigns. In Japan, for example, the official mascot of the 2019 World Cup, Ren-G, has been raising awareness among young people of the importance of rugby values such as respect and friendship, through educational workshops.

These funny, endearing characters are a reminder that rugby is not just an intense, competitive sport. Mascots add joy and levity, while symbolizing the unity between players and supporters. They are an essential part of rugby culture, bringing a smile and a touch of magic to every match.

Fact 22 - National team nicknames

In rugby, each national team has a unique nickname that reflects its identity and history. These nicknames are not chosen at random: they are often inspired by the country's culture, symbols or emblematic animals. They enable fans to identify even more closely with their team, and add a touch of personality to international competitions.

The All Blacks, the nickname of the New Zealand team, are perhaps the most famous. The name comes from the iconic black kit they've worn since the team's inception. But the nickname goes beyond color: it also evokes their power and unique style of play, which have made them a legend in the world of rugby.

In South Africa, the players are nicknamed the Springboks, after the fast, agile antelope that lives on the country's plains. This nickname embodies both the speed and endurance of the South African team, which has made rugby history with its victories, notably at the 1995 World Cup. The springbok is also a strong national symbol.

The Irish team is known as the Clover or Shamrocks, in reference to the three-leaf clover, a traditional Irish symbol. This nickname evokes luck, but also unity between the players, who represent both the Republic of Ireland and Northern Ireland. This team shows the importance of cooperation and overcoming divisions.

In Australia, the Wallabies are named after a typical Australian animal, a cousin of the kangaroo. Wallabies are known for their agility and resilience in the field, qualities that perfectly reflect the characteristics of this animal. The nickname is also a reminder of Australians' attachment to their unique wildlife.

Each nickname tells a story and strengthens the bonds between players and fans. These names are more than just labels: they embody the spirit and pride of each nation, giving rugby a unique cultural and emotional dimension. Whether you support the Blues, the Pumas or the Brave Blossoms, these nicknames symbolize the values of the team and the country they represent.

Fact 23 - Centenary clubs: history and tradition

In the world of rugby, some clubs have survived the decades to become veritable institutions. These century-old clubs, founded over a hundred years ago, carry with them a rich history and are the guardians of rugby's traditions. They embody the values of the sport, such as team spirit, loyalty and respect, while inspiring generations of players and supporters.

One of England's oldest rugby clubs is Blackheath RFC, founded in 1858. This London-based club played a key role in the development of modern rugby. In particular, Blackheath was involved in the creation of the first official rugby rules and was a founding member of the Rugby Football Union in 1871. Today, its story continues to fascinate.

Stade Toulousain is one of France's most famous century-old clubs. Founded in 1907, it is renowned for its impressive track record, with numerous French championship and European Cup titles. Toulouse fans, dressed in red and black, are proud of their club's heritage and its spectacular game, which has left its mark on the history of European rugby.

In New Zealand, the Canterbury Rugby Football Union, founded in 1879, is a symbol of the country's rugby history. The club has produced many of New Zealand's most famous players, the All Blacks. Their matches attract passionate supporters, who celebrate not only the victories, but also the club's tradition and commitment to the community.

In South Africa, the Western Province club, founded in 1883, is one of the pillars of South African rugby. Its history is closely linked to the development of rugby in the country, and its players have often worn the colors of the Springboks. This century-old club continues to be a major player in national competitions, with an intense and powerful style of play.

These century-old clubs are not just places where rugby is played. They are living memories of the sport, preserving tales of victories, challenges and memorable moments. Their stories show that rugby isn't just a game: it's a tradition that unites people, reminding them that commitment and passion are at the heart of the sport.

Fact 24 - Local derbies: high-voltage matches

In rugby, local derbies are matches between two teams from neighboring regions or from the same town. These matches are often the most eagerly awaited of the season, pitting not only clubs against each other, but entire communities against each other. The rivalry, sometimes decades old, turns each derby into a real battle, where the tension is palpable.

A famous example is the Basque derby between French clubs Biarritz and Bayonne. Located just a few kilometers apart, these two clubs share a rich history and a common passion for rugby. When they clash, the stadiums are packed with proud supporters, making the atmosphere electric and every action on the pitch decisive.

In England, the derby between Leicester Tigers and Northampton Saints is just as intense. These two clubs, who often dominate English rugby, battle for supremacy in the Midlands. The matches are renowned for their physical intensity and turnarounds. The rivalry doesn't stop on the pitch: it extends to the fans, who sing and cheer their teams on with fervor.

South African derbies, such as those between the Bulls and Stormers, add an even more physical dimension. The players, often from the same rugby schools, know each other well, making each confrontation even more personal. These matches are marked by a formidable intensity, where every tackle, every scrum, becomes a declaration of superiority.

Local derbies are not just sporting competitions. They are also cultural celebrations, where supporters express their regional pride. Traditions such as special songs and pre-match meals strengthen the bond between clubs and their communities. Every derby is a party in which everyone takes part, from the players to their families.

These high-tension matches are a concentration of what makes rugby so special: passion, commitment and the importance of local roots. Local derbies are a reminder that rugby isn't just a global sport: it's also an affair of the heart, where the values of belonging and healthy rivalry take on their full meaning.

Fact 25 - Summer touring: international challenges

Summer tours are key moments in the international rugby calendar. Every year, during the summer, national teams from the northern hemisphere travel to the southern hemisphere to take on formidable opponents. These matches measure the strengths of the teams and offer an intense spectacle, with each nation proudly defending its colors.

These tours have a long history. The first international tour dates back to 1888, when British players traveled to New Zealand and Australia for a series of matches. Although rudimentary by today's standards, the trip laid the foundations for the international confrontations that captivate millions of spectators today.

Summer tours are a unique challenge for European teams. They take place in different conditions, often in intense heat and against teams from the southern hemisphere at the height of the season. The All Blacks, Springboks and Wallabies are renowned for their dominance at home, making every win by a visiting team particularly precious.

A memorable moment occurred in 1971, when the British and Irish Lions completed a historic tour of New Zealand. They became the only team to beat the All Blacks in a series of test matches on home soil. This success left a lasting impression and remains an example of the strategic and emotional importance of these tours.

These matches are not just sporting challenges, but also cultural encounters. Players discover local traditions, such as the haka of the All Blacks or the war dances of the Pacific Islands. The passionate local fans create a unique atmosphere in the stadiums, making each match unforgettable.

Summer tours are a real test for teams, but they also embody the essence of rugby: respect for opponents, the discovery of new cultures and the opportunity to showcase talent on a world stage. They are a reminder that this sport, though intense, remains a celebration of human values and the bond between nations.

Fact 26 - The evolving rules of rugby

Rugby, as we know it today, is the result of a constant evolution of its rules. The sport, which originated in English schools in the XIXe century, saw its first rules formalized in 1845 at Rugby School. Back then, the game was very different, with no real referees and much more brutal contact than today.

One of the first major developments was the introduction of the trial as the principal means of scoring points. Originally, try-outs were not scored directly. They only offered the possibility of kicking to score. It wasn't until 1891 that tries began to be worth points, rapidly becoming the heart of the attacking game.

The rules have also evolved to make rugby safer and fairer. For example, high tackles, which endanger players, have been banned. Similarly, the rules governing scrums and rucks have been modified to reduce injuries. The introduction of yellow and red cards has made it easier to penalize dangerous or unsportsmanlike behavior.

Another key moment in the history of rugby rules was the appearance of the professionals in 1995. Prior to this date, rugby was strictly amateur, and players were not paid a salary. This change led to an overhaul of certain rules to make the game faster and more spectacular, in order to attract more spectators and sponsors.

The rules have also been adapted to take account of technological advances. Video refereeing, introduced in the 2000s, has made it possible to review contentious actions such as tries or serious fouls. This innovation has improved the fairness of the game and reduced refereeing errors, although it remains a subject of debate among fans.

The evolution of the rules shows that rugby is a living sport, capable of adapting to the times while preserving its fundamental values. Every change, whether it concerns safety, fairness or the spectacle, aims to make the game fairer and more exciting for players and spectators alike.

Fact 27 - Equipment: from leather to synthetics

Rugby players' equipment has come a long way since the early days of the sport. In the past, balls, jerseys and boots were made from simple materials such as leather and cotton. Today, technological advances have transformed this equipment to enhance players' performance while guaranteeing their safety.

In the early days, rugby balls were made from inflated pigs' bladders encased in leather. These balls were heavy and irregular, making them difficult to handle, especially in wet weather. Players had to adapt to unpredictable bounces. It wasn't until the 1980s that lighter, water-resistant synthetic balls became the norm.

The jerseys have changed too. Initially, they were made of thick cotton, designed to resist pulling during matches. But this material, though robust, became very heavy when wet. Modern jerseys, made from synthetic fibers, are lightweight, breathable and snug-fitting, enabling players to run faster and reduce catching by opponents.

Rugby boots, once made of hard leather with rudimentary studs, have also evolved. Today's models are designed to offer optimum grip on different terrains, while being lighter and more comfortable. Cleats are interchangeable, enabling players to adapt to different playing conditions, whether dry or muddy.

Player safety has also been improved thanks to modern equipment. Mouthguards, essential for preventing jaw injuries, are now custom-molded for optimum comfort. Helmets and shoulder pads, made from shock-absorbing materials, protect players without restricting their movements, a crucial balance in such an intense sport.

These advances show just how much rugby has adapted over time. Every innovation, whether it concerns balls, clothing or protective gear, aims to make the sport safer, faster and more spectacular. They are also a reminder that behind every match lies a fascinating blend of tradition and modernity.

Fact 28 - Cleats: grip and performance

Cleats are essential for rugby. They enable players to remain stable on the pitch, accelerate and change direction quickly, even in difficult conditions. Much more than just shoes, they are designed to optimize performance while ensuring safety, especially on muddy or slippery terrain.

The first rugby cleats, back in the XIXe century, were rudimentary. They were made of thick leather and fitted with metal studs, fixed directly into the sole. These models offered good grip, but were heavy and uncomfortable. Over time, materials evolved to become lighter, while offering better protection for the feet.

Today's studs are made from synthetic materials that combine lightness, strength and comfort. The soles are fitted with plastic or metal studs, often interchangeable. This allows players to choose the length of studs according to the type of terrain: short for dry ground and long for muddy ground.

Cleats also play a strategic role in the game. A forward, who spends a lot of time in the scrum, will prefer sturdy studs for greater stability. A winger, on the other hand, will opt for lighter studs to maximize his speed during sprints. Each position therefore has its own specific needs, and equipment is designed to meet them.

Leading brands work with professional players to constantly improve their models. For example, cleats with flexible soles cushion impacts and reduce the risk of injury. These technological innovations show just how crucial attention to detail is in this sport.

Cleats are more than just tools: they are a direct link between the player and the field. They symbolize the adaptability and precision needed to excel at rugby. Whether it's a tackle, a sprint or a scrum, studs are an invisible but essential part of every decisive action.

Fact 29 - The jerseys: iconic colors and designs

Rugby shirts are more than just clothing. They represent a team's identity, with colors and designs that tell a story. These emblematic outfits, worn with pride by players and supporters alike, embody the passion and unity that characterize the sport.

Originally, the first rugby shirts were made of thick cotton, designed to withstand the violent pulls and contacts of the game. Colors were often chosen according to local availability, which explains why many clubs adopted simple stripes or patterns. Over time, these choices became visual signatures for each team.

Some national teams are instantly recognizable thanks to their iconic jerseys. New Zealand's All Blacks, for example, wear a plain black outfit, a symbol of their strength and elegance. This simple yet powerful color choice has become a globally recognized symbol, intimidating their opponents even before the match begins.

In France, Les Bleus wear royal blue shirts, reflecting the national colors. This hue, associated with the country's history, lends a patriotic dimension to the team's matches. The fans, often also dressed in blue, create a sea of color in the stadiums, reinforcing the connection between the team and the public.

Clubs also have their own distinctive designs. Stade Toulousain, for example, is known for its red and black shirts, which symbolize fighting spirit and passion. These colors, handed down from generation to generation, recall the club's values and traditions, while inspiring respect and admiration.

Today's modern jerseys don't just look good: they're also designed to enhance player performance. Made from lightweight, breathable materials, they allow great freedom of movement while resisting pulls and impacts. These innovations show how tradition and technology come together in rugby.

Wearing a rugby jersey, whether you're a player or a supporter, is an act of pride. These garments tell a unique story, associated with victories, challenges and memorable moments. Shirts are not just uniforms: they are living symbols of rugby's passion and values.

Fact 30 - Referees: guarantors of the rules of the game

Referees play an essential role in rugby. They are not only there to whistle for fouls, but also to ensure that the game runs smoothly, that teams play fairly and that players are safe. Respect for them is a fundamental value in this sport, where their authority is rarely challenged.

Rugby referees wear distinctive uniforms, often in bright colors, to make them easy to spot on the pitch. They use a whistle to signal infractions and carry a microphone to communicate with players and assistants. This helps to explain their decisions and maintain transparency at critical moments.

In addition to the main referee, two linesmen watch over the sides of the pitch. Their role is to signal when the ball is out of play, fouls outside the central referee's field of vision, and to assist in situations such as conversion kicks. Effective coordination between these officials is essential to ensure smooth game management.

Rugby has introduced video refereeing, also known as TMO (Télévision Match Officiel), to review complex actions or contentious tries. This system helps to make the right decisions at decisive moments, such as a disputed try or dangerous play. This technological innovation underlines rugby's commitment to fairness and safety.

Some referees have become iconic figures thanks to their charisma and expertise. Nigel Owens, for example, is known for his clear communication style and subtle humor. His decisions, always made with firmness and respect, have made him one of the most respected referees in rugby history.

Being a rugby referee requires not only an excellent knowledge of the rules, but also the ability to handle pressure. Each decision can influence the course of a match, but their role goes beyond results: they embody the values of rugby, showing that respect and fairness are at the heart of the sport.

Fact 31 - Rugby balls: evolution and manufacture

The rugby ball is a unique element that sets this sport apart from others. With its characteristic oval shape, it offers unpredictable and spectacular play. But this ball, which seems so familiar today, has undergone many transformations since its beginnings to become the high-performance object that players use.

The first rugby balls were made from inflated pigs' bladders, covered with hand-sewn leather. These balls had an irregular shape, influenced by the natural size and shape of the bladders. They were heavy and impractical, but their uniqueness already contributed to rugby's originality from other sports.

Over time, manufacturing improved. At the end of the XIXe century, pig bladders were replaced by rubber inner tubes, standardizing the ball's shape. The oval shape, although slightly rounded at the time, was retained as it offered advantages for passing and rebounding. The balls were also lighter and easier to handle.

Today, rugby balls are made from synthetic materials such as polyurethane. These materials make the balls weather-resistant, enabling them to maintain a firm grip even in the rain. The rough surfaces of modern balls are designed to improve grip, helping players to catch and handle them in action.

Ball size and weight are now regulated to ensure fairness in competitions. An official ball is approximately 28 centimetres long and weighs between 410 and 460 grams. It must also meet precise rebound and durability criteria. These strict standards ensure a balanced game at all levels.

Each ball tells a story, from its manufacture in specialized factories to its use on the pitch. Some balls become famous, like the one used in World Cup finals, where they are engraved with specific details. These balls, witnesses to historic moments, symbolize the passion and ongoing evolution of rugby.

Fact 32 - Club anthems: fan songs

Supporters play an essential role in rugby, and nothing symbolizes their passion better than club anthems. These songs, sung in unison by thousands of voices in the stadiums, are much more than mere melodies. They carry the soul of the teams, unite the fans and create a unique atmosphere that makes every match memorable.

Every rugby club has its own anthem, often inspired by local history or culture. Stade Toulousain, for example, is famous for its emblematic song, "Se Canto", a traditional Occitan song. Toulousain fans sing this song with fervor, transforming the stadium into a veritable sea of sound that galvanizes the players.

In England, Leicester Tigers also have a very popular anthem: "Tigers, Tigers, Burning Bright". Inspired by a poem by William Blake, this song is a reminder of the fans' attachment to their team's history and traditions. At every match, it resonates throughout the stadium, giving the players extra energy.

Club anthems are not just about cheering. They are also symbols of identity and pride. Supporters of Ulster in Ireland sing "Stand Up for the Ulster Men", an anthem that celebrates their region and their team. This song becomes particularly moving during great victories or difficult moments.

These songs are often accompanied by specific gestures or rhythms. Fans of the Scarlets in Wales, for example, bang drums to accompany their anthem, creating a festive, rhythmic atmosphere. This interaction between fans and team strengthens the bond between players and fans.

Anthems transcend the pitch. They are taken up at celebrations, in pubs and even by the fans themselves. These songs become family traditions, handed down from generation to generation. They remind us that, in rugby, every victory and defeat is shared, not just by the players, but by an entire community.

Club anthems are much more than just melodies. They embody the collective spirit, pride and passion of rugby. At every match, their echo in the stadiums tells a unique story, uniting players and fans in the same fervor.

Fact 33 - Barbarians tours: spirit of the game

The Barbarians, or Baa-Baas, embody the pure spirit of rugby. This unique team, founded in 1890 by William Percy Carpmael in England, brings together guest players from various clubs and nations. It is famous for its attacking style of play, based on fun and creativity. Playing for the Barbarians is considered an exceptional honor for any rugby player.

Unlike traditional teams, the Barbarians have no home ground or championship to contend with. They only get together for friendly matches and tours. Their motto, "Play, Fun and Friendship", perfectly sums up their philosophy: to play rugby in a spectacular way, while respecting the fundamental values of the sport.

A legendary moment in the history of the Barbarians came in 1973, when they took on the All Blacks at Cardiff Stadium. This match is often regarded as the greatest ever played, thanks in no small part to a try scored by Gareth Edwards after a series of extraordinary passes. The try illustrates the daring and team spirit that characterize the Barbarians.

Barbarians tours are also opportunities for cultural encounters. As they travel around the world, the players discover new traditions and share unique moments with their opponents. This blend of competition and camaraderie makes the Barbarians a symbol of rugby unity.

To be invited to join the Barbarians, it's not enough to be an excellent player. Human qualities such as respect, humility and team spirit are just as important. The Barbarians are looking for players capable of playing with panache, but also of integrating into a multinational team in just a few days.

The Barbarians are a reminder that rugby is first and foremost a game, where fun and friendship must come first. Their spectacular tours and matches offer a welcome break from rigorous competition, celebrating the essence of rugby: a sport where the spirit of sharing and creativity must never be forgotten.

Fact 34 - Record stadium crowds

Rugby is a sport that brings huge crowds together, and some matches have broken impressive attendance records. These moments, when tens of thousands of fans gather in the same stadium, testify to the incredible passion this sport arouses. Each spectator, with his or her chants and cheers, contributes to the unique energy that reigns at these events.

One of the most impressive records was set in 2000 during a match between New Zealand and Australia at Sydney's Stadium Australia. On that day, 109,874 fans attended the thrilling encounter. The stadium, built for the Olympic Games, offered enormous capacity, enabling this event to make rugby history.

In Europe, matches in the Six Nations Tournament regularly draw huge crowds. The 80,000-seat Stade de France is often packed to the rafters for French team matches. For example, a match between France and England in 2011 drew record crowds, proving just how important this tournament is to fans.

Rugby isn't confined to traditional stadiums. At the 2015 World Cup in England, a match between Ireland and Romania was played at Wembley, a stadium usually reserved for soccer. The match attracted over 89,000 spectators, setting a record attendance for a Rugby World Cup, demonstrating the growing universality of the sport.

In the southern hemisphere, matches between the Springboks and the All Blacks are particularly popular. The Ellis Park stadium in Johannesburg is often packed to the rafters during these matches. During the 1995 World Cup final, the stadium welcomed over 60,000 fans in an electrifying atmosphere, immortalized by the Springboks' historic victory.

These record crowds show that rugby is much more than a sport: it's a real social phenomenon. The packed stadiums symbolize the unity of the fans, their pride in their teams and their love of the sport. Each record-breaking match becomes an unforgettable celebration, where emotion transcends the simple result of the game.

Fact 35 - The longest rugby matches ever played

Rugby, an intense sport by nature, has seen matches last far longer than the regulation 80 minutes. These marathon matches, often organized for special events, are tests of the players' physical and mental endurance. They push back the limits of the sport, while providing impressive spectacles for spectators.

One of the longest matches in history was played in England in 2011, in Chippenham, Wiltshire. For 24 uninterrupted hours, two local teams battled it out to set a world record and raise money for charity. Each player had to overcome fatigue and sore muscles to stay on the pitch.

Another memorable match took place in South Africa in 2014. It lasted 26 hours and 35 minutes, bringing together passionate fans in a collective effort to beat the previous record. The players showed incredible courage, supported by fans who cheered them on relentlessly, despite the difficult conditions.

To organize such matches, specific rules are put in place. Teams are often made up of a large number of players, who take it in turns to allow breaks and avoid injuries. Referees, too, have to be replaced regularly to maintain their vigilance and guarantee fairness throughout the match.

These extraordinary matches are not just sporting feats. They often serve to raise funds for important causes or draw attention to social issues. For example, the record-breaking match in 2011 helped fund projects to help disadvantaged children, showing that rugby can be a powerful force for solidarity.

Rugby's longest matches are a reminder that the sport is about much more than results. They embody endurance, teamwork and generosity. These marathon encounters, though rare, remain engraved in the memories of all those who take part, whether players, referees or supporters.

Fact 36 - The biggest comebacks

Rugby is a sport where everything can change in a matter of minutes, and the greatest comebacks are the proof. These unforgettable matches, in which a team manages to turn around a desperate situation, embody the fighting spirit and magic of the sport. Each spectacular turnaround is a lesson in perseverance and teamwork.

One of the most famous examples took place during the 2012 European Cup. Stade Toulousain, trailing Racing 92 27-3 at half-time, managed to score 28 points in the second half to win 31-27. This legendary match shows how a team, even in difficulty, can find the strength to surpass itself and show solidarity.

In 2003, another landmark match pitted the British Barbarians against the South African Springboks. After trailing by 22 points, the Barbarians scored a series of spectacular tries to finally snatch victory. This match has gone down in history as an example of the bold, creative play that characterizes the Barbarians.

At the 2019 Six Nations Tournament, Scotland also pulled off a memorable comeback against England. Trailing 31-0, the Scottish team scored six consecutive tries to come back to 38-38, in what remains one of the most thrilling matches in the competition's history. The explosion of joy from the Scottish fans showed just how exceptional this turnaround was.

Score rallies are not just a feature of international competitions. In regional leagues and local clubs, there are many similar stories of teams refusing to give up despite large point differentials. These moments strengthen the bonds between players and fans, united in their passion for the game.

The great comebacks remind us that rugby is much more than just a sport of points and scores. They celebrate the spirit of resilience and show that, until the final whistle blows, anything is possible. These sometimes unexpected feats are etched in the memories of players and fans alike.

Fact 37 - The most capped players in history

In rugby, to be "capped" means to have played an international match for your national team. The most capped players in history have left their mark not only on their nations, but also on world rugby through their longevity, talent and dedication. These athletes have played one match after another, writing a unique page in the history of the sport.

Richie McCaw, legendary captain of the All Blacks, is one of the most capped players of all time. With 148 caps between 2001 and 2015, he led New Zealand to two World Cup victories. His leadership, ability to read the game and exemplary work ethic have made him a respected figure on and off the field.

Welshman Alun Wyn Jones is also a rugby monument. With over 150 caps to his name, he has become a mainstay of the Welsh team. Known for his toughness and fighting spirit, he has played a key role in several Six Nations Tournament victories. His consistency and determination are admired by all his team-mates.

In women's rugby, England's Rochelle Clark holds the record for most caps with 137. Nicknamed "Rocky", she embodied the power and passion of the England team for over ten years. Her commitment to developing women's rugby is as important as her exploits on the field.

South Africa's Victor Matfield, an iconic second row, has 127 caps to his name. Known for his touch dominance and tactical awareness, he helped the Springboks win the World Cup in 2007. His influence is not limited to the field: he has inspired many young players to follow in his footsteps.

These players embody the perseverance and love of rugby. Through their exceptional performances and longevity, they have left an indelible mark on the sport. Each of their matches was a demonstration of their passion, reminding us that rugby is not only a physical affair, but also one of the heart.

Fact 38 - The youngest and oldest international players

In the history of rugby, some players have stood out for their age at the time of their first or last international selection. Whether very young or very old, these athletes prove that rugby can welcome talent of all ages, provided they have the courage and passion to represent their country.

The youngest player to play an international match was Alfred "Alfie" Pugsley, a Welshman who played for his national team in 1888, at just 16 years and 356 days old. He was still only a teenager when he took on grown-up men on the pitch. His appearance, though rare, remains an example of a time when player ages varied more widely than they do today.

In the modern era, George North, another Welsh star, also made his debut at a very young age. At just 18, he scored two tries against South Africa in his debut match in 2010. This impressive debut heralded a brilliant career, making him one of the best wingers of his generation.

At the other extreme, some players have pushed back the boundaries of age in international rugby. Diego Ormaechea, Uruguay's captain at the 1999 World Cup, made history by playing a match at the age of 40. This veteran, who combined his role as a player with that of a veterinarian in everyday life, remains an emblematic figure in South American rugby.

In New Zealand, Colin Meads, nicknamed "Pinetree", also played a key role right up to the end of his career. Although not as old as Ormaechea, his longevity and consistency are admired by generations of fans. His physical strength and experience have made him a pillar of the team.

These players, whether young prodigies or experienced figures, illustrate the diversity of rugby's career paths. Each has contributed his or her own energy, wisdom or enthusiasm to the history of the sport. Their age, though exceptional, has never been a barrier to their talent and passion for rugby.

Fact 39 - Rugby families: sporting dynasties

In rugby, certain families pass on their passion for the game from generation to generation, creating veritable sporting dynasties. These families, where several members have worn the same national jersey or played at a high level, embody the love of rugby and the spirit of camaraderie that goes with it. For them, rugby is a family affair.

In New Zealand, the Whitelock family is emblematic. Four brothers - George, Sam, Adam and Luke - have all played professional rugby, with Sam becoming an All Blacks star. Their story is one of siblings united by a common passion, and their exploits are a reminder that New Zealand rugby is also rooted in family values.

South Africa also boasts a legendary family: the Du Plessis. Brothers Jannie and Bismarck played together for the Springboks. Jannie as prop and Bismarck as hooker, they formed a formidable duo in the scrum. Their complicity on the pitch is the perfect example of what brothers can achieve together in this sport.

In France, the Spanghero family is another outstanding example. Brothers Walter, Claude, Guy and Laurent all played rugby at a high level. Walter, the most famous, became a mainstay of the French national team in the 1960s and 1970s. Their name remains etched in the history of French rugby, synonymous with strength and determination.

Wales is not to be outdone by the Quinnell family. Derek Quinnell represented his country in the 1970s, and his sons Scott and Craig followed in his footsteps. Scott, in particular, has become a Welsh legend thanks to his power and charisma. Their story is one of a family passion for rugby, passed down from father to son.

These families don't stop at the pitch. They also inspire future generations, showing that the values of rugby - respect, effort and teamwork - can be passed on in the home. Their influence goes beyond sporting results, leaving a lasting legacy in the world of rugby.

Rugby families are living examples of the impact of sport on family ties. Their passion, talent and dedication remind us that rugby is much more than just a game: it's a tradition, a heritage and a celebration of human values.

Fact 40 - Players scoring after a delayed whistle

Rugby, with its precise rules, sometimes offers unexpected moments when tension is at its height. One of the most spectacular is when players score points after a delayed whistle. This kind of action arises from the referee's advantage, allowing play to continue despite a previous foul. These moments often mark a decisive turning point in a match.

A famous example took place during the 2019 Six Nations Tournament, when Scottish winger Darcy Graham scored a memorable try against England. Although a foul had just been called against the English, the referee gave the Scots the lead. Graham seized the opportunity to run between the defenders and score the try, transforming the momentum of the match.

The All Blacks, renowned for their instinct and responsiveness, have also provided such moments. In a test match against Australia in 2015, Beauden Barrett intercepted a ball after a delayed whistle. Exploiting the advantage left by the referee, he scored a decisive try, demonstrating the importance of playing to the end, even in complex situations.

The delayed whistle is not just an opportunity for attackers. It can also add pressure to the defense, forcing players to react quickly while avoiding further fouls. This demands total concentration from all parties, making every second crucial in these phases of the game.

These actions, though short-lived, are a reminder that rugby is a sport of intelligence and strategy. Players must read the game, anticipate the referee's decisions and seize every opportunity. It also illustrates the importance of communication on the pitch, where a simple signal from the referee can transform a defensive situation into a scoring opportunity.

Points scored after a delayed whistle are not just technical feats. They are a testament to the spirit of rugby: to play boldly, to trust your team-mates and to never give up until the action is over. These moments are often etched in our memories, reminding us just how unpredictable and captivating this sport can be.

Fact 41 - Amateur players turned professionals

Rugby has evolved from a purely amateur sport to a professional discipline, but some players have marked this transition by rising from the fields of local clubs to reach the top. These stories, marked by hard work and passion, show that talent can be found anywhere, even far from the spotlight of major competitions.

New Zealand icon Jonah Lomu began playing rugby at school before becoming a global phenomenon. Spotted for his power and speed, he impressed right from his debut with the All Blacks in 1994. His dazzling career, although cut short by health problems, shows how an amateur player can shake up the codes of the sport.

In France, Sébastien Chabal is a perfect example of a player who rose from the local game to international stardom. A native of Valence, he began his career with regional clubs before establishing himself as a formidable force in the French national team. His famous beard and aggressive style of play have made him a fixture in stadiums the world over.

The Pacific Islands have also produced many talented players, often from modest backgrounds. Fiji-born Semi Radradra, for example, started out playing in his village before moving on to the major international competitions. His meteoric rise testifies to the immense reservoir of talent in this part of the world.

The transition from amateurism to professionalism, made official in 1995, opened up new opportunities for these players. Professional leagues such as the Top 14 in France and the Premiership in England have enabled them to turn their passion into a career. These competitions offer the ideal terrain for developing their skills and gaining recognition.

These inspiring stories are a reminder that rugby is above all a matter of passion and perseverance. Each amateur player who reaches the top embodies the fundamental values of the sport: respect, collective effort and surpassing oneself. Their stories are a source of motivation for all young people who one day dream of following in their footsteps.

Fact 42 - The most expensive transfers in rugby

In the world of professional rugby, player transfers from one club to another are sometimes accompanied by impressive sums of money. These transactions reflect the importance of players to the success of teams. Although less publicized than in other sports, some transfers in rugby have left their mark in terms of both cost and stakes.

One of the most famous transfers is that of Charles Piutau. This New Zealand player, a former All Black, left Wasps to join Bristol in 2018. His contract, valued at almost a million euros a season, made him one of the highest-paid players in rugby. Piutau was known for his spectacular performances and versatility on the pitch.

In France, the Top 14 is renowned for attracting top international talent. Dan Carter's transfer to Racing 92 in 2015 was a landmark moment. The two-time world champion from New Zealand signed a multi-million euro contract, bringing his experience and exceptional talent to a club in search of titles. He went on to help Racing win the championship.

The English are not to be outdone. Player Sam Burgess, famous for his career in XIII rugby, was recruited by Bath Rugby in 2014 for a significant fee. Although his move to XV rugby was short-lived, his transfer showed the growing interest of clubs in attracting players from different rugby disciplines.

South African rugby, known for its raw talent, has also seen players leave for lucrative contracts. Bryan Habana, one of the fastest wingers in history, signed for RC Toulon in 2013 for a hefty fee. His signing strengthened the team, which dominated the European scene for several seasons.

These transfers show the extent to which clubs are willing to invest in players capable of making a difference. The sums involved, though impressive, reflect the value of talent and the impact these players have on the pitch. Each transfer tells a unique story, where strategy and passion intertwine.

Fact 43 - Famous injuries and triumphant returns

In rugby, a demanding sport where contact is intense, injuries are part and parcel of many players' careers. Yet some of them have made spectacular comebacks after difficult ordeals. These stories of resilience and triumph show the mental and physical strength needed to shine again at the highest level.

England legend Jonny Wilkinson has often been hampered by injury. In 2003, after leading England to the World Cup with his legendary drop-goal, he was forced to take several months off the field due to shoulder problems. Despite this, Wilkinson came back stronger, becoming a model of perseverance and helping RC Toulon win several European titles.

South Africa's Schalk Burger has been through much more than a sports injury. In 2013, he contracted bacterial meningitis, an illness that could have ended his career. After a long recovery, he returned to the field, proving that nothing could dampen his passion for rugby. His return to the national team was acclaimed by the whole world.

Paul O'Connell, Ireland's famous captain, has also overcome many challenges. Suffering a serious hamstring injury at the 2015 World Cup, he had to leave the tournament prematurely. Although his international career ended there, his return to action with Munster showed his immense determination.

In France, Florian Fritz, emblematic center for Stade Toulousain, has lived through moments marked by spectacular injuries. In 2014, after an impressive concussion, he returned to the field with a courage hailed by his teammates. Although his safety was sometimes debated, his love of rugby remained evident.

These stories remind us that rugby is not only a sport of strength, but also of the heart and mind. Every return to the field, after physical or personal hardship, is a victory that inspires teammates and supporters alike. These players embody the spirit of rugby: never give up, even in the face of the greatest challenges.

Fact 44 - Players who have successfully changed sport

Some rugby players have talents that go beyond the pitch. Many of them have switched sports and gone on to shine in a different discipline. These spectacular transitions show the extent to which rugby develops physical and mental qualities that can be used in other sports.

Sonny Bill Williams, a famous New Zealand player, is a striking example. Not only did he excel in XV and XIII rugby, he also became New Zealand's heavyweight boxing champion. Known for his power and versatility, he juggled these two sports with remarkable success, inspiring many youngsters to follow in his footsteps.

Jarryd Hayne, a talented Australian rugby XIII player, decided to try his luck in American soccer in 2015. He joined the San Francisco 49ers, an NFL team, and quickly impressed with his speed and agility. Although he later returned to rugby, his time in the NFL proved his adaptability.

In England, Mike Catt, a former rugby international, showed astonishing skills in cricket during his youth. Before devoting himself entirely to rugby, he played the sport at a high level, combining qualities of endurance and precision that also served him well on the rugby pitch.

In women's rugby, Ellia Green, a former Australian rugby sevens player, has successfully reconverted to athletics. A specialist in sprints, she has taken part in several international competitions. Her explosive speed, which made her a formidable winger, has become an essential asset on the track.

These sporting transitions are not only due to their exceptional physical talents. Rugby players also develop an iron mentality and a sense of team spirit, qualities that are indispensable in all sports. Their success in other disciplines shows that rugby trains complete athletes, capable of adapting and performing in a variety of contexts.

The stories of these players are a reminder that sport is a land of infinite opportunities. Their journeys prove that the qualities acquired in rugby can open unexpected doors, transforming their passion for the game into a much wider adventure.

Fact 45 - Legendary coaches and their philosophies

Coaches play a crucial role in the success of rugby teams. Some have become legends thanks to their unique ideas, innovative strategies and ability to inspire their players. These iconic figures have left their mark on rugby history, transforming ordinary teams into winning machines.

Graham Henry, nicknamed "Ted", led the All Blacks to victory at the 2011 World Cup. His philosophy was based on fast, accurate play, with an emphasis on players' mental well-being. He believed that happy athletes play better, an idea that has revolutionized coaching approaches in modern rugby.

In France, Jacques Fouroux, nicknamed "le Petit Caporal", made his mark on the national team in the 1980s. Although not tall, his vision of the game was immense. He popularized evasive rugby, where speed and agility took precedence over brute force. This approach led France to several memorable victories in the Five Nations Tournament.

Eddie Jones, renowned for his exacting standards and strategic thinking, has transformed several national teams, including England and Japan. With Japan, he orchestrated a historic victory over South Africa at the 2015 World Cup, showing that even "small" nations could topple rugby's giants thanks to meticulous preparation.

Clive Woodward, England's 2003 World Cup-winning coach, is another example of a visionary coach. He introduced technological and scientific tools to analyze the game, a first in rugby. His method has enabled England to develop formidable discipline and efficiency on the pitch.

These coaches don't just draw up strategies. They are leaders, capable of rallying their teams around a common vision. They teach life lessons as important as those on the pitch: perseverance, respect and self-confidence. Their legacy inspires not only their players, but also future generations.

Legendary coaches show that rugby isn't just about muscles. It's a sport where thought, innovation and humanity play roles as vital as strength and speed. Their philosophies remain models, proving that good leadership can change the course of history.

Fact 46 - Women's teams: growth and success

Women's rugby is experiencing spectacular growth worldwide. From its humble beginnings, the sport has become a field of success for many players and teams, demonstrating that rugby is not just for men. Women's teams embody the values of passion, courage and solidarity that define the sport.

New Zealand's Black Ferns are a shining example of success. With several World Cup titles to their name, they often dominate their opponents thanks to their impeccable technique and team spirit. Their victory in 2017, when they beat England in the final, remains a historic moment for women's rugby.

In Europe, the England team, nicknamed the Red Roses, are renowned for their power and discipline. In 2014, they won their second World Cup by beating Canada. This triumph is the fruit of a structured program that encourages the development of young players and promotes the practice of rugby from an early age.

France is no exception. Les Bleues, known for their spectacular play, rival the world's best teams. Their victory over the Black Ferns in the 2018 Autumn Tests marked a turning point, proving that they can beat the best. The Women's Six Nations Tournament, which they play every year, is a key platform to showcase their talent.

Women's rugby also continues to grow, thanks to international competitions. The World Cup and the Olympic Games, where Rugby VII was introduced, have brought new stars to the fore. New Zealand's Portia Woodman, for example, has become an icon thanks to her speed and spectacular tries.

Federations are increasingly investing in women's rugby, creating academies and leagues to develop talent. In South Africa, Japan and the USA, programs are emerging to encourage female participation. These initiatives show that women's rugby is booming and gaining worldwide recognition.

Women players and teams are pushing the boundaries of rugby, inspiring entire generations. They remind us that rugby is a universal sport, where everyone can shine if they work hard and believe in their abilities. Their journey is a lesson in determination and collective success.

Fact 47 - The smallest players in history

Rugby is often associated with big, powerful players, but some of the sport's greatest moments have been achieved by small players. Their agility, speed and intelligence have enabled them to surpass expectations and establish themselves among rugby's giants.

Fumiaki Tanaka, a Japanese scrum-half measuring just 1.66 meters, is one of these exceptional players. Known for his speed and precision, he made history by becoming the first Japanese to play in the prestigious Super Rugby with the Highlanders in New Zealand. His key role in Japan's historic victory over South Africa in 2015 proved that size is no limit.

Another outstanding example is Cheslin Kolbe, a South African winger measuring 1.71 meters. His small stature has not prevented him from becoming one of the most feared players in modern rugby. In the 2019 World Cup final, he scored a spectacular try against England thanks to his lightning speed and unpredictable hooks. Today, he is considered a role model for smaller players.

In France, Clément Poitrenaud, although slightly taller (1.80 m), was often considered small for a professional player. This fly-half left his mark on French rugby with his vision of the game and his ability to create opportunities, even against larger opponents. His elegant play and precision are his hallmarks.

In the 1980s, Gareth Edwards, the 1.73-meter Welsh scrum-half, left an indelible mark on rugby. His speed and strategic thinking led the Welsh team to numerous victories. Today, he is recognized as one of the greatest rugby players of all time.

These players prove that rugby is not just about brute strength. Their success is based on qualities such as speed, technique and creativity. They embody the idea that talent and determination can overcome all barriers, reminding us that in this sport, the heart is sometimes more important than the body.

These inspirational figures show all young players that size doesn't matter if you want to succeed in rugby. Their journeys illustrate the essence of the sport: surpassing oneself, teamwork and passion, no matter what the challenges or physical differences.

Fact 48 - The fastest match tries

Rugby is a sport where every second counts, and some players have made history by scoring incredibly fast tries. These spectacular moments demonstrate the importance of concentration from the kick-off, and the ability to exploit opponents' mistakes immediately.

In 2017, in the English Premiership, Lee Blackett scored a try after just 8 seconds of play. Playing for Wasps, he seized the opportunity of a ball poorly recovered by the opposing team just after kick-off. This feat is remembered as a perfect example of responsiveness and determination.

In international rugby, France holds an impressive record thanks to Vincent Clerc's try in a 2007 match against Italy. In less than 20 seconds, Clerc broke through the Italian defense after a quick combination of the French back lines. The try showed just how creative Les Bleus could be in surprising their opponents in the early stages of the game.

In rugby sevens, where speed is king, even faster tries are often scored. South African rugby legend Cecil Afrika scored a try in just 7 seconds at a tournament in Hong Kong. Taking advantage of a perfectly-adjusted kick-off, he sped past the whole defense to put the ball behind the line.

Quick tries are not just a question of individual talent. They also reflect the perfect coordination between a team's players. A striking example is the All Blacks, masters of strategy, who scored a lightning try against England in the 2019 World Cup thanks to a pinpoint combination between their forwards and backs.

These moments illustrate the beauty of rugby: a surprise can happen at any moment. Players and teams capable of scoring so quickly show that agility, intelligence and tactical preparation are essential to turning unexpected opportunities into memorable feats.

Fact 49 - The longest international careers

Rugby, a demanding sport for body and mind, rarely sees players maintain their top level for many years. Yet some exceptional rugby players have managed to prolong their international careers, becoming models of endurance and resilience.

One of the most impressive records belongs to Welshman Alun Wyn Jones. This emblematic second row made his debut in 2006 and went on to play over 150 games for Wales. His longevity is based on rigorous preparation and exemplary discipline. In 2021, he again took part in a tour with the British and Irish Lions, showing that he was still at the top of his game.

All Blacks legend Richie McCaw played 148 international matches between 2001 and 2015. Known for his mental strength and ability to play through injury, he led his team to back-to-back World Cup victories in 2011 and 2015. His influence on the game and his consistency make him a role model for players the world over.

Italy's Sergio Parisse is another example of longevity. Making his debut in 2002, this number 8 wore the Italy jersey for almost two decades. Even when the Italian team was struggling to compete with the big nations, Parisse remained an inspiration, thanks to his talent and dedication.

South Africa's Victor Matfield, an imposing second row, enjoyed an exceptional career, playing for the Springboks between 2001 and 2015. Even after a three-year break, he returned to international level to help his team. His tactical intelligence and touch control made him an indispensable player.

These players show that longevity in rugby doesn't just depend on luck or genetics. It's based on meticulous preparation, an unwavering passion for the sport and an ability to adapt to the changing demands of the game. Their careers inspire young players to strive for excellence throughout their careers.

Long international careers are also a reminder of the importance of respect for team-mates and opponents. By staying at the highest level for so long, these players have left their mark on rugby through their consistency and love of the sport, becoming legendary figures for entire generations.

Fact 50 - The drop goal: a decisive kick

The drop goal is one of the most spectacular and strategic moves in rugby. It consists of bouncing the ball on the ground before kicking it between the opposing posts. This kick earns three points, a precious advantage in tight matches.

One of the most memorable drop goals was scored by England opener Jonny Wilkinson in the 2003 World Cup final against Australia. With only a few seconds remaining in the match, Wilkinson pulled off the perfect drop-goal to give his team victory. The moment has become the stuff of legend, showing just how much this gesture can change the outcome of a match.

To succeed with a drop goal, the player must combine precision, concentration and speed. Under pressure from the opposing defense, he must find the right moment to attempt his shot. A well-adjusted pass from his team-mates is often essential to create the opportunity. The drop goal is often used when other offensive options are blocked.

Historically, the drop goal has been a central feature of rugby, particularly before tries became more important over the years. In the early decades of the game, teams relied more on this move to score points. Today, it remains a formidable weapon, used at key moments to surprise opponents.

The great players capable of mastering this technical gesture are often forwards or scrum-halves. However, some forwards, such as New Zealand's Zinzan Brooke, have astonished the world with spectacular drop goals. Brooke scored a drop goal from almost 40 meters during the 1995 World Cup, a rare feat for a player in his position.

The drop goal embodies the beauty and strategy of rugby. Combining individual technique and team coordination, it reminds us that every detail counts on the pitch. These decisive moves, often made under immense pressure, remain etched in fans' memories, adding a touch of magic to this exciting sport.

Fact 51 - Players who have scored in more than one World Cup

Scoring a try in the World Cup is a feat that few players can claim. But some rugby players have managed to score tries in several editions of this prestigious competition, demonstrating not only their talent, but also their longevity on the international stage.

South Africa's Bryan Habana is one of the most famous players to have scored at several World Cups. Habana, a fast and powerful winger, scored tries in the 2007, 2011 and 2015 editions, equaling Jonah Lomu's record of 15 tries scored in the finals. His performances helped South Africa win the title in 2007.

New Zealand legend Jonah Lomu also scored in two World Cups, in 1995 and 1999. In the 1995 competition, Lomu stunned the world with his spectacular tries, particularly against England. His power and speed were unrivalled, and he remains a role model for young players.

England's Jonny Wilkinson, although famous for his kicking, has also scored tries in several World Cups. He contributed to England's successes in 1999, 2003 and 2007, most notably in the 2003 final, where he played a decisive role in his country's title win.

In the southern hemisphere, Australians David Campese and Drew Mitchell also made their mark, scoring tries at several World Cups. Campese, known for his feint passing and creativity, left an indelible mark in the 80s and 90s, while Mitchell shone with his attacking flair in the 2000s.

These players demonstrate that scoring in several World Cups is not just a question of talent, but also of preparation, discipline and love of the game. They embody the very best of rugby: the ability to respond at crucial moments, in front of millions of spectators around the world.

Fact 52 - Grand Slam winning teams

In European rugby, the Grand Slam is an extraordinary feat. It is won by a team in the Six Nations Tournament when it beats all the other teams in the same edition. To achieve this feat requires a combination of talent, discipline and iron will.

England is the team with the most Grand Slams. Their historic victories include such highlights as the 2003 Grand Slam, the year they also triumphed in the World Cup. With legendary players such as Martin Johnson and Jonny Wilkinson, England dominated that year, imposing their powerful, precise style.

Wales, another great rugby nation, has also enjoyed several memorable Grand Slams. One of the most famous was in 1971, when a team featuring stars such as Gareth Edwards and Barry John shone. Their fluid play and collective spirit inspired generations of Welsh fans.

France, with its unique flair, has also etched its name in the history of the Grand Slams. In 1997, Les Bleus, led by Philippe Saint-André, seduced the world with their inventive and daring rugby. This Grand Slam consolidated their reputation for creating magical moments on the pitch.

Ireland, though rarer in this category, has celebrated some impressive Grand Slams, most notably in 2009. Under the leadership of captain Brian O'Driscoll, the Irish won their first Grand Slam since 1948, a milestone for Irish rugby.

Although Scotland has not won a Grand Slam recently, it remains proud of its past achievements, particularly in the early decades of the Tournament. Scottish Grand Slams are a reminder of their historic strength in the sport.

The Grand Slam is not just a series of victories. It's a declaration of superiority in one of rugby's oldest and most prestigious competitions.

Fact 53 - Matches played with historical equipment

Rugby as we know it today has evolved considerably, but some teams and competitions have decided to pay homage to history by playing matches with historic equipment. These encounters are not just spectacular: they are a reminder of the sport's roots and traditions.

In the 2000s, a friendly match in England saw two teams wearing thick cotton shirts, similar to those used in the late 19th century. These jerseys, far from being as breathable as today's, were heavy and often uncomfortable when wet. Modern players, accustomed to synthetic materials, had a glimpse of the challenges faced by their predecessors.

The balls used in these historic matches were also different. Made of genuine leather, they were much heavier, especially in wet weather. Controlling the ball was a real challenge, as it became slippery and difficult to handle. These matches highlight the mastery of the players of yesteryear, who played with much less high-performance equipment.

Cleats were also very different. At one time, shoes were made of stiff leather, without modern technologies for comfort or grip. During matches with historic equipment, modern players were able to experiment with these rudimentary studs, which were often uncomfortable and impractical on wet pitches.

These special matches don't just recreate the equipment. Sometimes, they also adopt the rules of the time, such as scrummaging where players organize themselves differently, or touches played without alignment. These adjustments show just how much rugby has evolved in terms of technique and strategy.

These encounters are popular with spectators, who discover an almost forgotten rugby, and with players, who can experience the history of the sport in an immersive way. These events are also an opportunity to highlight the technological advances and resilience of the players of yesteryear.

By playing with historic equipment, modern players pay tribute to those who marked rugby's beginnings. These matches are bridges between the past and the present, reminding us that, while the game may evolve, its spirit remains unchanged.

Fact 54 - Teams with midnight matches

Playing a rugby match at midnight may seem strange, but some teams have done it, transforming the pitch into a unique nocturnal theater. These matches, often organized for special occasions, capture the imagination of players and spectators alike.

In 2013, an unusual rugby match took place at midnight in New Zealand to celebrate the arrival of the New Year. The match kicked off exactly at midnight, with fireworks lighting up the sky. The players, dressed in brightly patterned jerseys, put on a magical show, combining the passion of rugby with the excitement of the festivities.

Playing at night requires special organization. The pitches are lit by powerful floodlights to provide optimum visibility. However, lighting cannot replace natural light, and players have to adapt to new conditions. These matches demonstrate the flexibility of athletes, capable of performing even in unusual circumstances.

Night matches can also have symbolic implications. In 2000, a match played at midnight in South Africa paid tribute to coal miners, whose working hours often prevented them from attending daytime matches. This gesture strengthened the bond between local clubs and their communities.

For spectators, attending a match at midnight is an unforgettable experience. Chants and cheers echo through the night, creating a different atmosphere from traditional matches. The fatigue and effort of the players is even more impressive under the artificial lights.

These night matches show that rugby, beyond the rules and techniques, is a celebration of sport and solidarity. To play at midnight is to push back the limits of what is possible, proving once again that this sport is much more than just a game.

Fact 55 - Matches played on unusual pitches

Rugby, with its demanding rules and specific needs, is usually played on grass pitches. However, some matches have been played in surprising locations, proving the adaptability and creativity of rugby players.

A memorable match took place in 2015 on a beach in Wales. Sand replaced grass, completely changing the style of play. Players had to redouble their efforts to move around and avoid sinking. This physical challenge made the game as fun as it was spectacular for spectators.

In the mountains, rugby has also conquered new heights. In Switzerland, a match took place on a glacier at an altitude of over 2,000 meters. Equipped with special crampons, the players faced not only their opponents, but also the bitter cold. The match underlined their resilience and raised awareness of climate change.

Another unusual pitch was an aircraft carrier. In 2009, to promote rugby to the military, a match took place on the deck of a warship in Australia. The limited space and hard ground made passing and dodging even more technical, offering a unique challenge for the participants.

Some matches were played in the heart of forests or in natural settings. In New Zealand, a friendly match was organized on a meadow surrounded by giant trees, providing a magical setting. The spectators, seated on logs, were close to the action.

These unusual matches show that rugby can adapt to a variety of environments while retaining its competitive spirit. They are a reminder that the sport is not confined to a standard pitch, but can flourish wherever passion takes it.

Fact 56 - Teams who played with underdogs

Playing 15 against 15 is the norm in rugby, but sometimes teams are faced with the challenge of carrying on with one or more players missing. This can happen after a red or yellow card, or because of injury when all the substitutes have already been used.

One of the most famous stories dates back to 2007, during a match between Wales and Australia. The Welsh played an entire game with just 13 players due to two injuries. Despite being outnumbered, they showed remarkable courage to score a late try.

In 2014, the All Blacks also made their mark. Playing with just 14 players after one of their own was sent off in the first minute, they pulled off a victory over South Africa. Their discipline and strategy were hailed the world over.

Amateur teams are not to be outdone. During a match in England, one team finished with 11 players after a series of expulsions and injuries. Against all the odds, they heroically defended their end line and prevented their opponents from scoring until the final whistle.

Numerical inferiority often pushes the remaining players to outdo themselves. They have to run harder, stick together more and sometimes even change the way they play to compensate for absences. These situations make for memorable matches, full of suspense and emotion.

These feats illustrate the spirit of rugby: fighting to the end, even in the face of adversity. They show that collective intelligence, courage and determination can make up for much more than numbers.

Fact 57 - Matches decided by kicks after extra time

In some rugby matches, when no team manages to break the deadlock after regulation time and extra time, the outcome is decided by a series of kicks. These moments are intense and demand extraordinary concentration from the players.

One of the most memorable examples took place in 2009, during the European Cup final between Leicester and Cardiff Blues. After extra time had ended in a draw, victory came down to penalties. Under immense pressure, the players had to convert penalties, until Leicester prevailed.

The principle is simple: each team chooses shooters from among its players, even those not used to the task. Penalties are struck from specific positions on the pitch, and each miss can cost the team victory.

These kicking sessions are rare in rugby, but they create unforgettable memories. Players have to deal not only with the technique of kicking, but also with the weight of responsibility, because their team-mates are counting on them.

For spectators, these moments are filled with emotion. Each kick can turn defeat into triumph or hope into disappointment. Stadiums hold their breath with every shot, making the atmosphere electric.

These matches show that, in rugby, victory depends not only on strength and speed, but also on composure and precision. They remind us that even the smallest actions can have a huge impact.

Fact 58 - Players who have played for two different nations

It is rare, but not impossible, for a player to represent two nations in rugby. These situations arise thanks to specific eligibility rules, often linked to changes of nationality or periods without playing for the national team.

A famous example is Frank Bunce, who played for Samoa before becoming a mainstay of the All Blacks. His switch from one team to the other has left a lasting impression, testifying to his exceptional talent, capable of shining under two different jerseys.

In recent history, World Rugby rules have allowed this change under certain conditions, such as a long period without representing a nation or direct family ties with another country. These rules aim to preserve fairness while giving players opportunities.

These players often bring a wealth of different styles and strategies, derived from their experience in two different rugby cultures. This can also strengthen the team they join, thanks to their versatility and adaptability.

For fans, seeing a player they admire in another team may come as a surprise, but it illustrates the international and inclusive nature of rugby. It's also proof that the sport can unite nations around a common passion.

These situations remind us that rugby is more than a sport: it's a worldwide community. The players who cross these borders embody this idea, showing that whatever jersey they wear, their love of the game remains the same.

Fact 59 - Teams with back-to-back titles

Winning a rugby title is an achievement in itself, but keeping it is even more impressive. It requires constant discipline, relentless strategy and a close-knit team. Teams that achieve this feat leave a lasting mark on the history of rugby.

New Zealand's All Blacks are famous for their consistency. They won back-to-back World Cups in 2011 and 2015, an exceptional record in such a demanding competition. Their precise play and team spirit are the keys.

In Europe, Wales has shone by winning the Grand Slam in the Six Nations Tournament on several occasions, notably in the 1970s. This dominance over several years testifies to the quality of the players and coaches of the time.

South Africa has also enjoyed consecutive memorable successes in other tournaments. The Springboks showed their strength in the World Cup and Rugby Championship, beating the world's best teams on several occasions.

France marked the history of European rugby with consecutive victories in the Five Nations Tournament before the switch to six teams. These triumphs helped build France's reputation as a rugby powerhouse.

These winning streaks are not confined to the big nations. A number of lesser-anticipated teams have also pulled off feats in local and regional competitions. They show that, in rugby, anything is possible with determination and talent.

These dynasties of champions remind us that continued success requires endurance, hard work and a strong desire to win. These teams inspire not only their fans, but also future generations of players.

Fact 60 - Tackling: technique and safety in action

Tackling is one of the most spectacular moves in rugby. It's also a crucial means of stopping an opponent. But it's not a matter of rushing in at random. Successful tackling requires technique, composure and, above all, respect for the rules to ensure the safety of the players.

A good tackle starts with the correct position. The player should bend his knees, keep his head to one side to avoid any direct impact, and aim for the waist or legs. This keeps the opponent off balance without causing injury. Coaches teach players these gestures right from the start.

The rules prohibit high tackles, i.e. those that touch the neck or head. These actions are dangerous and severely punished. In an international match, a player may receive a yellow or red card for an illegal tackle. These measures protect athletes' health.

Rugby stars such as Richie McCaw and Siya Kolisi were renowned for their efficient, clean tackles. They demonstrated that technique and game intelligence are far more important than brute force. A good tackle is above all a considered gesture.

Equipment also plays a role. Mouthguards and shoulder pads reduce the risk of injury. However, players must always follow technical instructions to avoid dangerous impacts. Safety depends above all on respect for the gestures taught.

A well-executed tackle is a moment of bravery and efficiency. It's not just a question of blocking the opponent, but of doing it in the spirit of rugby: with respect, technique and great attention to safety. That's what makes this gesture as impressive as it is noble.

Fact 61 - Largest point spreads in the finals

A rugby final is often synonymous with suspense, but some have been distinguished by impressive point spreads. These matches remain etched in history, not only for their score, but also for the incredible performances of the winning teams.

In the 2001 European Cup final, Leicester Tigers beat Northampton Saints 34-0, a monumental margin for such an event. It was a match in which the Tigers dominated, and every move seemed unstoppable, leaving their opponents with no answer.

Another landmark final was the 1998 Super Rugby final. The Crusaders crushed the Highlanders with a final score of 49-18. This match demonstrated the total mastery of the New Zealand team, which combined speed, power and tactics to perfection.

Even in national championships, some of the gaps in the final are impressive. In France, Stade Toulousain won a crushing 26-0 victory over Perpignan in 2008. The match highlighted Toulousain's defensive rigor and offensive ingenuity.

In these finals, the gaps often reflect superior preparation, in-form key players and infallible strategy. Dominant teams take advantage of every opponent's mistake to score crucial points, making the gap even more striking.

However, these gaps do not diminish the value of the losing teams. Reaching a final is already an achievement. These matches remind us that in rugby, the level of competition is always high, and every point scored is the fruit of an immense collective effort.

Fact 62 - Matches with the most tries

Some rugby matches remain famous for their abundance of spectacular tries. These matches offer an unforgettable spectacle, as players compete in speed, agility and ingenuity to cross the end line.

In 1995, during the World Cup, New Zealand crushed Japan with a record score of 145-17. The match is remembered for the 21 tries scored by the All Blacks, including several by the legendary Jonah Lomu.

Another legendary match pitted Australia against Namibia at the 2003 World Cup. The Wallabies scored 22 tries in a 142-0 victory. This performance reflected incredible collective control and a relentless determination to score at every opportunity.

In Super Rugby, the Crusaders and Lions made history with a 16-try match in 2016. This explosive duel captivated spectators with its intensity and frenetic pace, where each team attacked relentlessly, creating constant suspense.

Known for their attacking spirit, Barbarians matches often feature impressive scores. In 1973, their match against New Zealand in Cardiff saw 9 tries, some of them spectacular, like the one by Welshman Gareth Edwards, considered the finest in history.

These matches show the essence of rugby: a game where the pleasure of attacking and scoring tries is at the heart of the action. Every try scored is a celebration of individual talent and collective effort, turning these matches into unforgettable celebrations for players and spectators alike.

Fact 63 - Players who have scored all their team's points

In the history of rugby, a few exceptional players have achieved the rare feat of scoring all their team's points in a match. These moments highlight their precision, endurance and ability to shine under pressure.

At the 1995 World Cup, French opener Thierry Lacroix scored all 19 of his team's points against Scotland. With penalties and conversions, he single-handedly carried the weight of the scoreline, giving France a crucial victory.

Jonny Wilkinson, famous for his role in England's 2003 title triumph, has also achieved this feat several times. His ability to kick accurately and penetrate opposing defenses has made him a formidable player. In 2002, he scored all 21 of England's points against New Zealand.

Another famous player is Naas Botha, the legendary South African striker. In international matches, he often scored all his team's points with his powerful, precise kicks, leaving opponents unanswered.

This feat is not limited to the backs or openers. Some forwards like Zinzan Brooke, thanks to their attacking prowess and precision on foot, also scored all their team's points, proving that in rugby, every position can be decisive.

These unique performances are a reminder that in a team sport, one player can sometimes take over and become the hero of a match. But even in these individual exploits, strategy and the support of team-mates remain essential to making these memorable moments possible.

Fact 64 - Teams having won all their matches on a tour

Winning every match on a tour is a rare feat, demonstrating a team's total domination in a competition or against several opponents. This type of performance will go down in rugby history as an example of collective excellence.

New Zealand's All Blacks are famous for achieving this feat on several occasions. In 1924, their tour of Europe saw them win all their matches, earning them the legendary nickname of "The Invincibles". They have beaten national teams and local squads without faltering.

The British and Irish Lions, a team featuring the best players from England, Scotland, Wales and Ireland, have also enjoyed triumphant tours. In 1974, when they visited South Africa, they won all but one of their matches, which ended in a draw - an impressive record.

South Africa also shone on their tours in the 1930s. In 1937, the Springboks toured Europe beating the continent's best teams, establishing their status as giants of world rugby. Their discipline and power were feared by their opponents.

Even lesser-known teams can achieve this feat. Fiji, for example, have won all their matches on regional tours thanks to their dynamic and spectacular style of play. These moments are a source of pride for emerging rugby nations.

These victorious tours mark not only the history of the teams, but also that of rugby as a whole. They are a reminder that, even far from home, these players transcend themselves to deliver unforgettable performances, etching their names in the annals of the sport.

Fact 65 - Longest interrupted losing streaks

In the history of rugby, some teams have gone through long periods of difficulty, accumulating defeats. But the moment they finally break that streak is often memorable, symbolizing perseverance and rebirth.

The Italians have long been perceived as the underdogs of the Six Nations Tournament. Between 2015 and 2022, they racked up 36 consecutive defeats. But in 2022, a victory over Wales in Cardiff put an end to that run. This match was marked by a spectacular last-minute try.

Samoa also went through a difficult period in the 2000s. After a series of defeats to major nations, their victory over Ireland in 2013 proved that they could compete with the best teams. This success inspired a revival in Samoan rugby.

In the 1990's and 2000's, Scotland suffered several years of defeat to England in the Six Nations Tournament. In 2000, they ended this losing streak with a memorable victory at Murrayfield. The jubilant Scottish public welcomed the moment as a national triumph.

Even emerging teams like Japan have had to overcome losing streaks at World Cups. Their historic victory over South Africa in 2015, after decades of setbacks, remains one of rugby's greatest moments. It was a feat that changed their status on the world stage.

These interruptions to long losing streaks are a reminder that, in rugby, anything can happen. Patience, teamwork and determination pay off in the end. These unexpected victories are not only moments of joy for the players, but sources of inspiration for their supporters.

Fact 66 - Players who have played in several professional leagues

Some rugby players have made history by playing in several professional leagues, exploring different sporting cultures while enriching their style of play. These careers are a testament to their talent and ability to adapt to the varied demands of world rugby.

Jonny Wilkinson, famous for his 2003 World Cup drop-goal, left England to play for RC Toulon in France. There, he conquered the Top 14 and won the European Cup several times, demonstrating that his talent transcended borders. His precision and rigor won over an international audience.

Dan Carter, another rugby great, has played in New Zealand, France and even Japan. After shining with the All Blacks, he enjoyed huge success with Racing 92 in France. Then he continued to dazzle fans in Japan with his elegant play and pinpoint passing.

Other players, like Australian Matt Giteau, have also crossed continents. After playing in Super Rugby, he joined the French Top 14, then the Japanese league. His experience and versatility have made him a star capable of playing in many different positions and styles.

The propensity to play in several leagues has also brought styles closer together. For example, South African players who join European clubs bring the power of southern hemisphere rugby. In return, they learn to play in different conditions, particularly in the rain.

These courses enrich not only the players themselves, but also their teams. Coaches use their experience to introduce new strategies. For young fans, they become examples of perseverance and openness to the world.

Fact 67 - Teams that have won titles in more than one country

Some rugby teams have achieved the feat of winning major competitions in several countries. This success requires not only talent, but also the ability to adapt to different styles of play and conditions.

RC Toulon is a prime example. This French club has repeatedly won the European Cup, a competition that brings together the best teams from several countries. With international stars like Jonny Wilkinson, they have conquered stadiums across the continent, proving their dominance beyond France.

The Crusaders, a legendary New Zealand team, have not only shone in Super Rugby, but also on international tours. By facing and beating teams from other continents, they have shown that their superiority is not limited to the southern hemisphere.

England-based Saracens have also made history, dominating the English Premiership and winning the European Cup. Their strength lies in a mix of local and foreign players, bringing complementary styles to triumph in different environments.

South African teams such as the Bulls have won prestigious Super Rugby titles against clubs from Australia and New Zealand. These successes demonstrate their ability to compete with the best teams in the world, even away from home.

These victories transcend borders, making these teams symbols of unity and global success. For young players, they inspire them to dream big and believe that, with hard work, it's possible to shine anywhere.

Fact 68 - Closed-door matches: reasons and impact

A behind-closed-doors rugby match means that spectators cannot attend. This can happen for a number of reasons: disciplinary sanctions imposed on a club or safety measures. For example, violent incidents in the stands may lead a federation to punish a team by holding its next match without an audience.

During the global pandemic of 2020, many rugby matches were played behind closed doors to protect the health of players and fans. Without the cheers and chants, the stadiums seemed eerily silent. The players, used to the energy of the crowd, had to draw on their personal motivation to stay focused.

Rugby without an audience isn't just different for the players. The referees hear the exchanges between players better, which can influence their decisions. It has also enabled TV viewers to better understand discussions between referees and captains thanks to the microphones.

Playing without spectators can also affect a club's economy. Tickets sold for a match are an important source of revenue. Behind closed doors, teams have to find other ways to compensate, such as TV broadcasts or partnerships with sponsors.

Nevertheless, some historic matches produced fine performances despite the absence of the public. For example, finals played under unusual conditions behind closed doors showed that the spirit of competition remained intact, even without the cheers in the stands.

For fans, not being able to cheer on their team at the stadium is a real ordeal. Yet even from a distance, their passion remains intact. Messages of support on social networks and banners in empty stadiums have become a new way of showing their love for rugby.

Fact 69 - Teams with memorable charity matches

Rugby is often much more than a sport: it's also a way of helping others. Teams have joined forces to play charity matches, raising money for important causes. A striking example was the one organized after an earthquake in New Zealand. The All Blacks played a selection of teams to collect donations for the families affected.

In England, the 2015 Rugby Aid Match brought together famous players and celebrities to support UNICEF. The well-attended match helped fund programs for children in need around the world. On the pitch, the players had a special energy, motivated not only by victory, but also by the idea of changing lives.

Some charity matches have a special atmosphere. At a match in South Africa, the Springboks took on a mixed team of former players. The proceeds were donated to an organization that fights poverty. The spectators, well aware of the objective, added to the fervor.

Charity rugby also goes beyond the boundaries of sport. At a match organized in France, professional and amateur players played side by side to fund medical research. These unique moments are a reminder that rugby never forgets the values of solidarity and generosity that characterize it.

Even small clubs are getting involved. One Irish club organized a 24-hour rugby marathon to raise funds for a local school. Players of all ages took turns on the pitch, showing that every gesture counts, no matter how small.

These matches are more than just competitions: they are testimony to the impact that rugby can have beyond the pitch. Players, supporters and organizers unite for noble causes, proving that rugby is above all a big family.

Fact 70 - Speed records in the field

Rugby is a sport where speed can make all the difference, especially when a player manages to outrun his opponents. One of the most impressive records is held by Carlin Isles, an American 7-a-side rugby player, who has been clocked at a speed in excess of 37 km/h. His speed earned him the nickname "the fastest man in rugby".

In rugby union, legendary South African Bryan Habana is often cited for his lightning speed. In one test, he was compared to a cheetah in a fictional race for an animal protection awareness campaign. But it wasn't just an act: Habana was capable of clocking speeds of 10.4 seconds over 100 meters.

Some lesser-known players have also made their mark through their speed. During a university match in New Zealand, an anonymous winger covered 80 meters in just a few seconds, dodging all his opponents. This kind of moment remains etched in the memories of spectators and inspires young players to work on their speed.

Speed isn't just about running in a straight line. Former England player Jason Robinson was famous for his dazzling changes of direction. His ability to accelerate in an instant while destabilizing his opponents made him a veritable nightmare to defend. He proved that speed combined with agility is a formidable weapon.

The forwards, generally larger in stature, can also be fast. Jonah Lomu, a colossus from New Zealand, could run at an astonishing speed for his size and weight. This combination of strength and speed enabled him to destroy opposing defensive lines, as he did at the 1995 World Cup.

These records show that speed in rugby is not limited to sprinters. It can take many forms, from phenomenal sprinting to unpredictable acceleration and unrivalled agility. Fast players are often the ones who turn games on their head at decisive moments.

Fact 71 - Players who inspire fictional characters

Some rugby players have left such an indelible mark on history that their lives or personalities have inspired fictional stories. The most famous example is Jonah Lomu, whose phenomenal power and speed have left such a mark that he has inspired heroes in popular sports comics.

In some countries, local players have inspired film and TV stories. Welsh legend Gareth Edwards, for example, was often cited as a source of inspiration for stories about ordinary heroes becoming champions. His exploits on the pitch, combining talent and modesty, made him perfect for fictional tales where perseverance and courage are at the heart of the story.

Entire teams have sometimes inspired stories. New Zealand's All Blacks, with their dominance and intimidating haka, have been used as models for imagining fictional teams with almost magical powers. These stories celebrate their discipline, strength and camaraderie, while capturing the imagination of young fans.

Some players with atypical characters have given birth to colorful characters. For example, the spirit and humor of Sébastien Chabal, nicknamed "The Caveman", have been reinterpreted to create eccentric heroes in humorous stories. His unique look and striking personality have made him an iconic figure.

Fictional tales inspired by rugby players are not limited to sporting exploits. The tenacity of players who have overcome difficult trials, such as injury or discrimination, has often provided the backdrop for stories of resilience and victory. These stories show just how much more rugby is than a sport: it's also a reflection of life.

These stories, sometimes exaggerated or idealized, introduce rugby to new generations, while celebrating the values that the sport embodies. The players' unique journeys inspire not only their teammates, but also thousands of young people who dream of following in their footsteps.

Fact 72 - Players who broke longevity records

Some rugby players have defied the test of time by playing at a high level well beyond the age when most hang up their boots. One of the best-known examples is Victor Matfield, a South African player who has continued to excel in international rugby well into his 38s, proving that experience and mastery can compensate for physical decline.

Another iconic player is Diego Ormaechea, the Uruguayan who made history by playing in the 1999 World Cup at the age of 40. This tireless captain led his team with courage, becoming the oldest player ever to take part in this prestigious tournament. His example has inspired many younger players.

Brad Thorn, a New Zealand player, also impressed with his longevity. He played until the age of 41, winning titles in several competitions. His secret lay in rigorous discipline and an unfailing love of rugby. His career, straddling XIII and XV rugby, demonstrated his incredible endurance.

Amateur players have also made their mark through their longevity. Some, like David Robinson in England, have played well into their 50s, taking part in local competitions while continuing to inspire with their passion. These examples show that the love of rugby can cross generations.

Longevity in this sport requires not only excellent physical condition, but also an ability to adapt. With the evolution of the rules and the increased intensity of matches, these players have been able to reinvent themselves and find ways to remain competitive. Their achievements command the respect of opponents and team-mates alike.

These longevity records are a reminder that rugby is not just about youth or brute strength. They show that mentality, experience and determination can prolong careers well beyond their expected limits. These players embody perseverance and dedication, core values of rugby.

Fact 73 - Teams having played matches on several continents

Some rugby teams have made history by playing matches on several continents, highlighting the sport's international reach. New Zealand's All Blacks, for example, are famous for their world tours, playing matches in Europe, Africa, Asia and America. These trips reinforce their status as global legends.

The Barbarians, a unique team made up of players of various nationalities, have also criss-crossed the continents, playing against local and national teams. During their tours, they played in South Africa, Australia, Argentina and even Asia, promoting the spirit of rugby wherever they went, and strengthening links between cultures.

After the end of apartheid, South Africa played on several continents to re-enter the international scene. Their participation in tours of Europe, Oceania and America was marked by memorable matches, such as their historic victory over England at Twickenham in 1997.

The British and Irish Lions, a team made up of players from the British nations, are famous for their international tours. They regularly play in South Africa, Australia and New Zealand, taking on local teams in iconic stadiums and creating rivalries that last for generations.

Some lesser-known teams have also crossed oceans to make history. Uruguay, for example, have played matches in Europe, America and Asia, often against much more powerful opponents. This has enabled them to gain experience and progress over the years.

These trips show that rugby transcends geographical boundaries. Playing on several continents requires teams to adapt to local climates, terrain and styles of play. These matches have enriched the history of rugby by uniting nations around a shared passion for this demanding and spectacular sport.

Fact 74 - Players who scored after intercepting passes

In rugby, intercepting a pass and running into the in-goal is one of the most spectacular moves. It requires perfect reading of the game, exceptional speed and great composure. These actions often occur just as the opposition is attempting a quick attack, offering the intercepting team an unexpected opportunity to score.

One of the most memorable moments of an interception occurred during a World Cup match, when South African player Cheslin Kolbe intercepted a decisive pass against Wales. Thanks to his speed, he covered the whole field to score a try to the applause of his team and the jubilant fans.

In 1999, Australia's George Gregan scored a crucial try after an interception in a semi-final match. It changed the course of the match in his team's favor. It showed how vigilant defense can turn an unfavorable situation into a decisive advantage.

Interceptions are not limited to major competitions. In amateur clubs and schools, talented players regularly perform this feat. These moments are often the most celebrated by their team-mates, as they combine surprise, intelligence and opportunism.

However, interceptions are not without risk. If the player misses the pass or is caught before reaching the in-goal, the opposing team can quickly recover the ball. This adds extra tension, as the player has to run at full speed while avoiding being tackled.

Tries after interceptions are a reminder that rugby is a sport where everything can change in a second. These spectacular gestures thrill the crowds and inspire young players to always remain alert and ready to seize their chance, even when victory seems remote.

Fact 75 - Players voted best player more than once

Being voted best player is a huge honor in rugby, but some exceptional players have been voted best several times. The title rewards their talent, determination and impact on the field. It means they have made an unforgettable mark on their era, season after season, inspiring their team-mates and impressing their opponents.

Richie McCaw, celebrated captain of the All Blacks, has twice been voted World Rugby Player of the Year. His exemplary leadership and ability to excel in decisive moments have made him a legend. These awards symbolize his domination of world rugby for many years.

Another player who shone was Dan Carter, also from New Zealand, twice crowned best player. Known for his precise play and strategic vision, he led his team to crucial victories. His mastery of both offensive and defensive phases remains a model for all ushers.

These multiple distinctions are not limited to the All Blacks. South Africa's Pieter-Steph du Toit also made history with his incredible performances. His power and hard work in rucks and mauls have often turned games in his team's favor.

These repeated awards underline not only the talent, but also the consistency of these players. To excel over many years in a sport as demanding as rugby is a remarkable feat. It requires intense training, a strong spirit and a great passion for the game.

Young players can learn from these champions that success comes with hard work and perseverance. Being voted best player several times shows that it's possible to push one's limits to reach even greater heights, even after an initial success.

Fact 76 - Players who have been coaches at the same time

Being both player and coach on a rugby team is a huge challenge. It requires you to manage both your own play on the field and the team's overall strategy. Yet some players have risen brilliantly to this dual challenge and left their mark on rugby history.

One famous example is Martin Johnson, who led the England team as player-coach for some matches before his retirement. Known for his determination and natural leadership, he motivated his team-mates while ensuring his personal performance at the highest level.

In New Zealand, All Blacks legend Colin Meads also played this dual role at times. His ability to assert himself on the pitch and make important tactical decisions enabled his team to keep performing at key moments.

At club level, this role has often been taken on by experienced players who know their team inside out. Gareth Edwards, for example, briefly fulfilled this dual role for Cardiff. His instructions as a coach were applied directly on the pitch, providing fluidity in the game.

Being a player and a coach at the same time demands a great deal of discipline. You have to manage your physical training while thinking about the best strategy for the team. This duality can be stressful, but it offers a unique insight into the game and the team's needs.

These cases are becoming increasingly rare as professional rugby evolves and specializes. However, they are a reminder of the importance of leadership and tactical intelligence in the sport. Player-coaches have left a valuable legacy, inspiring their teams to perform at their very best.

Fact 77 - Players who scored with unexpected combinations

In rugby, some spectacular actions are not born of brute force, but of incredible imagination. Players have scored memorable tries by exploiting unexpected combinations, defying the expectations of opponents and even spectators.

During an international match against Australia, the French team executed an unpredictable combination. The scrum-half, instead of sending the ball to his opener, passed it back to a prop who ran straight into the defense to score. Such a decision surprised everyone except his team.

The All Blacks are renowned for their innovations. During a Tri-Nations tournament, they deceived the South African defense with a quick touch feint. Rather than playing the traditional game, the ball was thrown low to a winger who was already sprinting. It was an audacious and precise try that left a lasting impression.

At club level, England's Harlequins are famous for their unusual tactics. One of their combinations includes cross-passing between forwards and backs, totally confusing the defense. This unconventional approach has enabled them to win tight games and entertain their fans.

Unexpected combinations require perfect coordination and lots of practice. They exploit speed, vision and the ability to take calculated risks. This blend of creativity and discipline shows just how strategic and physical rugby can be.

Trials like these remind us that sometimes thinking outside the box can make all the difference. These unexpected moments thrill crowds and remind us that rugby is not just a game of power, but also of intelligence and inspiration.

Fact 78 - Teams who have won major tournaments as underdogs

In the history of rugby, some triumphs have been totally unexpected. Teams described as "outsiders", often ignored by the experts, have managed to beat the odds to win prestigious tournaments. These feats show that determination and teamwork can overcome many obstacles.

In 1995, South Africa surprised the world by winning the World Cup. Having just returned to international competition after years of isolation, the Springboks were far from favorites. But thanks to solid play and incredible team spirit, they beat the All Blacks in the final, marking a historic turning point for their nation.

Japan also made history at the 2019 World Cup. Although they didn't win the tournament, the Brave Blossoms achieved a resounding feat by beating powerful teams like Scotland and Ireland. This extraordinary run enabled them to reach the quarter-finals for the first time.

The Argentine team also shone in 2007, when they came third in the World Cup. Regarded as challengers, the Pumas surprised renowned teams such as France. Their bold, disciplined style of play has won them worldwide recognition and inspired a new generation.

In the Six Nations, Italy have had their moments of glory by beating the favorites, proving that even developing teams can topple the giants. These unexpected victories are a reminder that rugby is a sport where anything can happen, especially when the heart and courage are there.

These feats are not just sporting achievements; they demonstrate the strength of character and unity of the teams. For fans, they offer unforgettable moments, proving that in rugby, the smallest can sometimes beat the biggest.

Fact 79 - Players who were captains at a young age

In rugby, becoming captain is an honor that demands leadership and maturity. Yet some players have taken on this role at a very young age, proving that they possessed these qualities long before their elders. Their example inspires generations and shows that age is no limit to responsibility.

Will Carling, one of England's most famous captains, was appointed at just 22 in 1988. His young age came as a surprise, but he proved his worth by leading his team to three victories in the Five Nations Tournament. His vision of the game and calmness under pressure left their mark on his era.

In New Zealand, Aaron Smith captained a provincial team at the age of 20 before joining the All Blacks. His nomination underlined his game intelligence and ability to inspire his teammates, even older ones. It shows that a good captain knows how to listen as well as how to lead.

In South Africa, Johann Heunis became captain of the Springboks at just 23 years of age. Despite his youth, he was able to unite his team and stand up to formidable opponents. His youth has not prevented his team-mates from respecting his decisions on the pitch.

France is no exception, with players such as Fabien Pelous, who captained his club at the age of 22 before taking charge of the national team a few years later. His youth has not prevented him from leading by example, displaying unshakeable determination.

Being a young captain requires great adaptability and a quick grasp of strategy. These players have proved that a leader can emerge at any age, as long as they have a passion for the game and respect for their team-mates. They remain role models for all those who dream of playing rugby.

Fact 80 - Rugby's biggest stars

Rugby is a sport for all sizes, but some players stand out for their impressive height or weight. These "giants" of the field don't go unnoticed and often use their extraordinary physique to change the course of a match, becoming key figures in the game.

Jonah Lomu, the famous New Zealand winger, was 1.96 m tall and weighed 119 kg. His power and speed were formidable, a rare combination that left its mark on rugby history. His opponents were hard pressed to stop him, even with several defenders on his tail, and he remains a global icon of the sport.

England's Martin Johnson, another rugby colossus, topped the 2.01 m mark. As captain of the England team, he led his country to victory in the 2003 World Cup. His size and strength enabled him to dominate scrums and command respect both on and off the field.

In modern rugby, French international Sébastien Vahaamahina impresses with his 2.03 m and almost 125 kg. His stature is an invaluable asset when it comes to tackling, where he excels, and his physical game is feared by his opponents. He is an example of the powerful forwards of the 21st century.

South African Bakkies Botha, 2 m tall and weighing 120 kg, was a mainstay of the Springboks for many years. His reputation as a tough, tireless player earned him the nickname "The Enforcer". His impact in the scrum and in the rucks was essential to his team.

These players demonstrate that physical size can offer incredible advantages in rugby, but their success is also based on talent and hard work. Rugby remains first and foremost a team sport, where heart and game intelligence are just as important as brute strength.

Fact 81 - Players selected after a position change

Some rugby players have succeeded in reinventing themselves by changing positions, demonstrating their versatility and adaptability. These changes, sometimes dictated by a team's needs or a player's physical characteristics, have often led to impressive careers.

Dan Carter, the legendary All Black, is a case in point. Before becoming the master opener, he began his career as a center. This repositioning enabled him to make full use of his vision of the game and his talent for kicking, making him one of the best players in history.

England star Jason Robinson also shone after a change. Initially a winger in XIII rugby, he was repositioned at the back in XV rugby. His lightning acceleration and ability to break through defenses made him an indispensable player in England's 2003 World Cup victory.

Another outstanding player is Australian George Smith. Originally trained as a winger, he was repositioned as a flanker. This change has benefited from his dynamism and ball-winning ability, making him a fixture on the international rugby scene.

Frédéric Michalak, a French player, has demonstrated a rare flexibility by alternating between the positions of opener and scrum-half. His dual skills have made him an invaluable asset to his team, particularly at decisive moments in major competitions.

These changes are never easy. They require hard work and an ability to learn new techniques. But they show that, in rugby, talent combined with effort can enable players to flourish where they are least expected.

Fact 82 - Matches played with customized balls

The rugby ball is much more than just a playing tool: it can also tell a story. At some memorable matches, specially customized balls have been used, adding a unique touch to these events and leaving a lasting impression on players and spectators alike.

For the 1995 Rugby World Cup, the ball featured a unique design to celebrate the event in South Africa. This special ball symbolized the unity and rebirth of a country that had just overcome apartheid. Spectators still remember it, not least because of the Springboks' victory.

For charity matches, balloons are often personalized with messages of support. One famous match in aid of medical research used a ball covered with celebrity signatures. The ball was auctioned off after the match, proving that rugby can also make a difference off the pitch.

In some historic tournaments, balloons bear the logos of the participating teams. At the Six Nations Tournament, for example, it's not uncommon to see balloons adorned with the emblems of the competing nations, adding a festive and symbolic note to these already exciting encounters.

Some teams also choose customized balls for special occasions. The Barbarians, for example, used a black and white ball in the colors of their famous jersey for a commemorative match. This unique ball reflected the spirit of this extraordinary team.

In tribute matches to rugby legends, the balls become symbols. A match dedicated to Jonah Lomu used a ball bearing his name and number. It was preserved as a precious souvenir of this event dedicated to a sporting giant.

These personalized balls add an emotional and visual dimension to the game. They transform a simple object into a symbol of history, culture and tribute, reminding us that rugby is much more than a sport: it's a collective memory.

Fact 83 - Matches played on unusual artificial pitches

Rugby, usually played on natural grass, has sometimes been played on artificial pitches. These unusual surfaces, sometimes chosen out of necessity or for special events, alter the experience of the game and offer unique memories for players and spectators alike.

One famous example is matches played in stadiums equipped with modern synthetic turf. These pitches, designed to withstand the elements, offer a uniform surface but change the feel of the game. Ball bounces are more unpredictable, adding an extra level of difficulty.

In places where the climate makes it impossible to maintain natural grass surfaces, artificial pitches are the only solution. In Russia, for example, some international matches were played on synthetic surfaces heated to prevent the ground from freezing. Players had to adapt to this significant difference.

Artificial pitches are also chosen for promotional events. During an exhibition match in a shopping mall in Asia, a synthetic pitch was installed especially for the occasion. The unusual setting attracted an uninitiated audience, giving a new boost to rugby's popularity.

In countries where green spaces are scarce, matches have been organized on synthetic surfaces installed in urban parks. These matches promote rugby in communities where it is not traditionally played, making the sport accessible to new players.

Artificial pitches can also play a role in sports innovation. Studies are being carried out to understand how these surfaces influence player performance and safety. Although some still prefer natural grass, these artificial pitches show that rugby can adapt to any situation.

Matches on unusual artificial pitches tell a story of adaptation and creativity. They prove that rugby, whatever the surface, keeps its spirit of competition and unity intact, captivating players and spectators around the world.

Fact 84 - Teams playing with fans in disguise

In rugby, fans play an essential role, and some choose to dress up to cheer on their team with even more creativity. These costumes add color and a unique atmosphere to the stands, making certain matches memorable both on and off the pitch.

At some international tournaments, such as the Six Nations, it's not uncommon to see stands packed with fans dressed up as historical figures, animals or superheroes. On one occasion, Welsh fans came dressed as dragons to symbolize their national emblem, creating an impressive atmosphere.

During a match in New Zealand, All Blacks fans chose to wear costumes depicting Maori warriors to honor the tradition of the haka. The players, inspired by this demonstration of cultural support, delivered an exceptional performance, marking the history of the match.

In local competitions, some fans adopt humorous disguises. A lower-division English team was supported by fans dressed as giant vegetables, a tribute to their club's unusual nickname. The cheerful energy of the crowd helped motivate the players.

Some costumes even have strategic meanings. In South Africa, a group of fans dressed up as zebras to symbolize the unity of different communities. Their message of peace and cohesion left a lasting impression well beyond the match.

These disguised supporters demonstrate that rugby is much more than just a sport. Thanks to their creativity, they bring crowds together and create memories that stay with players and spectators alike, adding a human and festive dimension to the game.

Fact 85 - Players selected in two different sports

Some rugby players are so exceptionally talented that they have been selected to represent their country in another sport. These versatile athletes, capable of shining in two disciplines, are often considered legends in the world of sport.

One of the most famous examples is Sonny Bill Williams. This New Zealand player was a star in both rugby union and professional boxing. His physical strength and coordination enabled him to rise to the top in these two very different sports.

In England, rugby player Jill Burns was a key figure. As well as playing for the women's rugby team, she also represented her country in athletics. Her speed on the rugby field was directly linked to her sprinting skills, which she used to score spectacular tries.

Transitions between rugby and cricket are not uncommon. South Africa's Jonty Rhodes, known for his exceptional cricketing talent, came close to pursuing a career in rugby. His speed and reflexes made him a valuable asset in both sports, although he ultimately chose cricket.

Australia's Ellyse Perry has done it again: she has played for the women's national rugby XV and soccer teams. This unique feat has made her an iconic figure in Australia, where team sports occupy a very important place.

These players embody the spirit of sport and the ability of effort to surpass limits. Their example shows that with hard work and passion, you can shine in many disciplines, inspiring generations of young athletes to push back their own boundaries.

Fact 86 - Teams that have used unprecedented defensive formations

In rugby, defensive strategies play a crucial role in preventing opponents from scoring. Some teams have revolutionized the game, inventing new and sometimes surprising formations that have left their mark on the sport's history.

The South African team, nicknamed the Springboks, introduced an ultra-aggressive lineout defense at the 2007 World Cup. This technique, known as "rush defense", involved moving forward quickly to stifle the opposing attack. It was so effective that it enabled the Springboks to win the tournament.

In 2015, the Samoa team surprised everyone with a defensive formation nicknamed the "moving wall". The players grouped together in a compact block that moved laterally, leaving very little space for the forwards. This strategy troubled many teams, even the most experienced.

The All Blacks, known for their creativity, also innovated with a double-curtain defense. A first line of players intercepted passes, while a second line handled tackles. This organization was used to great effect in many decisive matches.

In England, the Saracens club experimented with an inverted-V formation, where players retreated to give the illusion of an opening. This trap lured the attackers into an area where the defense could suddenly close in, often successfully.

These unprecedented defensive formations are not only impressive in their effectiveness. They also show just how much rugby is a sport where intelligence and adaptation can make all the difference, even against stronger or faster opponents.

Fact 87 - Matches played with guest referees

In rugby, referees play an essential role in ensuring compliance with the rules. There are matches where guest referees from other countries or sports have brought a special and sometimes unexpected touch to the game.

During a friendly tournament in New Zealand, a famous cricket referee was invited to direct a rugby match. Although he had to learn the basics of the rules quickly, his presence was greeted with enthusiasm. The moment strengthened the ties between the country's two iconic sports.

In South Africa, during a charity match between two professional teams, a soccer referee was chosen to officiate. His way of directing the game, based on soccer habits, added a touch of humor and conviviality to this unique encounter.

During a historic tour of France, an Australian team agreed to have the match refereed by a former local player turned amateur referee. The gesture was hailed as a mark of respect for the culture and traditions of French rugby, and the match is still remembered today.

In another famous case, a guest referee with an athletics background officiated a match in Scotland. Accustomed to running competitions, he was impressed by the speed and stamina of the players, while showing great rigor in applying the rules.

These moments show that rugby can be a sport of inclusion and sharing, even in the central role of the referee. These experiences enrich the game and remind us that rugby remains a place of creativity and openness, where team spirit sometimes transcends borders.

Fact 88 - Players who scored with unforeseen kicks

Rugby is a sport full of surprises, and some players have scored thanks to totally unexpected kicks. These actions demonstrate the importance of creativity and instinct in a game where every second counts.

During a match in New Zealand, a player, under pressure, attempted a back kick to move the ball away. To everyone's surprise, the ball bounced unpredictably and was recovered by a team-mate who ran straight into the in-goal to score a spectacular try.

In France, a third-row player executed a high kick, usually reserved for full-backs. The ball was misjudged by the opponents and landed directly in the hands of a winger, who had only to run for the try. The moment proved that audacity can turn a match around.

One of the most memorable kicks was attempted by a South African scrum-half. Instead of passing to his opener, he kicked over the defense. He recovered the ball himself, dodged a tackle and scored a try, leaving the crowd stunned.

In England, a forward took a low kick that seemed destined to gain ground. But the ball, deflected by an irregularity in the terrain, took a strange trajectory, allowing a center to seize it and score a decisive try.

Some players, like the ushers, are known for their precise kicking, but these actions are a reminder that even the least expected players can surprise. These unexpected moments are often the most appreciated by the fans.

These unexpected kicks underline the fact that rugby is a sport where nothing is ever decided in advance. Every player has a chance to shine, whether in the thick of the action or trying a risky move to change the course of the match.

Fact 89 - Teams with record consecutive wins

In the history of rugby, certain teams have marked their era by stringing together an impressive number of victories. These series are the result of rigorous discipline, collective talent and exceptional team spirit.

New Zealand's All Blacks hold one of the most impressive records with an 18-match winning streak between 2015 and 2016. This period includes their 2015 World Cup victory and test matches won against the world's best teams.

Another legendary series belongs to South Africa. The Springboks racked up 17 victories in the 1990s, a feat marked by their triumph at the 1995 World Cup, a historic moment for rugby and for their country.

In Europe, England also wrote a memorable page with 18 consecutive victories between 2015 and 2017. This run was capped by victory in the Six Nations Tournament, where they achieved a Grand Slam.

Women's rugby is no exception. New Zealand's women's team racked up an impressive series of victories in the 2000s, reinforcing their status as the best women's rugby team in the world.

Each series of victories shows the teams' ability to stay focused on their objective, despite the growing pressure to maintain their invincibility. These moments are etched in the memories of players and fans alike.

These feats are a reminder that in rugby, every match is a new challenge, but the great teams manage to maintain impressive consistency. These records are a testament to their greatness and lasting impact on the sport.

Fact 90 - Trials: key moments of the match

A try is the most exciting moment of a rugby match. It rewards creativity and teamwork. When a player flattens the ball behind the goal line, it triggers an explosion of joy among team-mates and fans alike.

Some tries become legendary. At the 1987 World Cup, Serge Blanco scored a decisive try in the semi-final against Australia. His sprint and determination led France to victory in a memorable match.

Tries are not always spectacular, but they can change the course of a match. A try scored from a powerful scrum or a well-constructed maul testifies to a team's strategy and collective strength.

Sometimes, tries are the result of long passes and frantic running. Jonah Lomu, New Zealand's famous winger, was known for his impressive tries where he cut through the defense like a tornado, scoring several times in the 1995 World Cup.

Trials are also a way of telling a story. At the 2003 World Cup, Jonny Wilkinson scored a crucial try in the final. The moment marked the history of English rugby and showed that a try can embody years of preparation.

Each essay bears the unique signature of its author. It reflects his vision of the game, his audacity and his ability to seize an opportunity. That's why tries are unforgettable moments for players and spectators alike.

Fact 91 - Matches played to celebrate historic anniversaries

Some rugby matches are played not just to win, but also to celebrate historic events. These special encounters recall landmark moments, bringing teams and fans together in a shared memory.

In 1995, a match was organized in New Zealand to commemorate 100 years of rugby in the country. The All Blacks took on a world selection. It was a unique moment when rugby legends shared the field to pay tribute to the sport.

In South Africa, a memorable match marked the centenary of the founding of the South African Rugby Federation in 1989. The match symbolized not only the history of rugby, but also the unity of a country still divided by history.

Some matches celebrate anniversaries linked to famous stadiums. In 2010, Twickenham, nicknamed the "House of Rugby", celebrated its 100th birthday with a spectacular match between England and Australia. Fans packed the stands to pay tribute to this iconic venue.

Sometimes these matches are not just a celebration, but also a way of supporting causes. In 2003, a match was played in Paris to commemorate the 50th anniversary of the Five Nations Tournament. Profits were donated to charity.

These matches are a reminder that rugby is more than just a sport. They celebrate the moments when history, culture and passion come together to create unforgettable memories for players and spectators alike.

Fact 92 - Matches played with mixed gender teams

Rugby is often seen as a physical sport, but it also knows how to bring men and women together on the same field in mixed matches. These encounters, often friendly or charitable, show that rugby is above all about collaboration and team spirit, whatever the strength or size of the players.

In 2015, a unique match took place in England where players from local clubs, both men and women, competed against each other in a festive atmosphere. The initiative aimed to promote equality in sport and encourage more women to join rugby, while reminding us of the importance of fair play.

The rules of these mixed matches are often adapted to avoid too much rough contact, but the intensity and commitment remain present. For example, at a tournament held in New Zealand in 2018, mixed teams showed that precise passing and strategy sometimes took precedence over raw power.

These matches also have symbolic significance. In South Africa in 2021, a mixed match was organized to celebrate Women's Day. It was a moving moment when male and female players wore special shirts together in tribute to this cause.

Beyond the rugby pitch, these mixed matches often inspire the younger generation. Schools in Australia have even integrated this practice into their sports activities to show students that cooperation between boys and girls can produce incredible results.

These mixed encounters are a reminder that rugby is more than a competitive sport: it's a tool for breaking down barriers, strengthening unity and proving that the game belongs to everyone, regardless of gender or origin.

Fact 93 - Players selected for unexpected moves

In rugby, some players have been selected thanks to unforeseen actions that have left a lasting impression on spectators and coaches alike. These gestures, often made under pressure or in decisive moments, demonstrate the instinct, creativity and courage needed to stand out on the pitch.

A famous example comes from a New Zealand player who, during an amateur match, intercepted a ball intended for a taller opponent. This daring move enabled him to score an impressive try and attract the attention of scouts, who promptly invited him to join a professional team.

Sometimes, these actions are not tries but technical gestures. In England, a young hooker was singled out for a particularly precise tackle that stopped a dangerous breakthrough. This moment, simple at first glance, revealed his ability to remain calm under pressure and to understand the game perfectly.

Spectacular kicks can also open doors. In Australia, a fly-half surprised everyone by landing a cross-kick from over 40 meters out, allowing his teammate to score. This kind of bold action shows a vision of the game that coaches are looking for.

In some cases, unexpected gestures are not only technical but also strategic. A South African player was spotted for his ability to motivate his teammates after a series of poor results. His natural leadership and team spirit convinced the coaches to give him a chance.

These selections show that, in rugby, it's often the spontaneous moments of genius that make the difference. Whether it's a perfect tackle, an inventive pass or an inspired gesture, these moments reveal unique talents capable of shining at the highest level.

Fact 94 - Games played to attract new spectators

In the history of rugby, certain matches have been organized specifically to attract new spectators. These often spectacular events aim to showcase the sport's unique qualities: intensity, team spirit and memorable moments that captivate even those who have never seen a match before.

A striking example is the friendly match organized in Dubai between a local team and international stars. Played in a modernized stadium, the aim was to promote rugby in a region where the sport was little known. The players' acrobatics and spectacular actions thrilled an often novice but conquered public.

In Argentina, a match was played in a public park to raise awareness of rugby among youngsters. The unusual pitch broke down barriers, making the game more accessible. At the end of the match, spectators were even invited to try out a few passes and tackles, reinforcing their connection with the sport.

In France, a night match was organized with special lighting and entertainment between periods of play. This innovative format attracted families and curious onlookers looking for a different experience. The children, in awe, often joined local clubs after attending these evenings.

In South Africa, a charity tournament saw school teams take on local stars. This unique mix inspired many young spectators. Seeing that even amateurs could shine on the pitch, some took a liking to rugby and decided to get serious about it.

These special matches prove that rugby has a unique ability to bring people together, whether novices or enthusiasts. By showcasing its energy and values, these events continue to turn spectators into fervent supporters of the oval ball.

Fact 95 - Players who scored after defensive errors

In rugby, some of the most memorable actions come from defensive errors. These unexpected moments highlight the speed and intelligence of players capable of transforming a defensive lapse into a decisive try. These feats are a reminder that rugby is a sport where every second counts, and where everything can change in an instant.

A famous example is a match between New Zealand and England, where an English defender, under pressure, attempted a desperate pass which was intercepted by an All Black. The New Zealand player, quick and responsive, ran over without being caught, scoring a try that changed the outcome of the match.

During a clash in the European championship, a ball poorly controlled by a full-back offered an unexpected chance to a winger. Taking advantage of the confusion, he grabbed the ball and ran between the posts, leaving the spectators stunned. This kind of action shows that staying alert is essential in this sport.

Defensive errors can also occur during scrums or rucks. A poorly managed throw-in can be recovered by a player from the opposing team, as in a historic match in South Africa, where a lightning-quick number 9 pounced on the opportunity to score.

Even the best teams are not immune to such mistakes. During a Six Nations tournament, a poorly negotiated touch left a gap for an Italian player. In the blink of an eye, he broke through the defense, leaving his opponents in disbelief. These unexpected moments add spice to the game.

Finally, these tries due to defensive errors remind us of an important truth: in rugby, you always have to play until the final whistle. Every player, whether attacker or defender, must be ready to take advantage of the unexpected, making every match a unique and captivating spectacle.

Fact 96 - Matches played with giant rugby balls

In the history of rugby, some special matches have been organized using giant balls to entertain spectators and test players' skills. These unusual encounters, often organized to coincide with festive or charity events, have transformed the game into an even more impressive and entertaining spectacle.

One of the most famous examples took place at a rugby festival in New Zealand. The players had to adapt to a ball twice their normal size. This enormous ball required special coordination, as it was difficult to grip and unpredictable in its bounces. Passing and kicking took on a totally new aspect.

In England, a charity match in support of an environmental cause used a giant ball made from recycled materials. Although it looked like a conventional ball, its imposing size forced the players to adopt novel, often hilarious tactics. The crowd laughed as scrums and touches were transformed into veritable balancing acts.

These matches are not just humorous; they also highlight the importance of teamwork. With a giant ball, it's almost impossible to play solo. Each player must rely on his team-mates to move this cumbersome and sometimes capricious object to the try-line.

In South Africa, a giant ball was used in a match to promote rugby among children. The young spectators were fascinated by the enormity of the ball and the way the players tried to master this leaping monster. This inspired many of them to want to try the sport.

These experiments show that rugby, even when played outside the traditional rules, remains a sport of coordination, agility and team spirit. The giant balls are a reminder that, sometimes, the unexpected and laughter are also essential elements of this game that fascinates so many people around the world.

Fact 97 - Matches played to promote sporting values

Rugby, as a team sport, has always been associated with values such as respect, solidarity and courage. Some matches have been specially organized to highlight these essential principles, transforming a sporting encounter into a real life lesson.

In Australia, a match between two amateur teams was organized to celebrate inclusion. Each team included players of different ages and backgrounds. This match showed that rugby can bring together very different people around the same passion. It was a moving moment, where team spirit was at the heart of the game.

In South Africa in the 1990s, a historic match was held to symbolize reconciliation after years of social tension. Pitting players from different communities against each other, the match demonstrated that rugby could be a powerful tool for uniting people despite their differences, while sharing values of mutual respect.

Another striking example comes from France, where a school tournament was organized to teach fair play. Referees explained the rules to the children during the games, and teams were rewarded not only for their victories, but also for their behavior. Young players learned to respect their opponents and appreciate the game as a whole.

In New Zealand, a match was played to promote courage in the face of hardship. The players were former sufferers of serious illness or injury, returning to the pitch after long personal struggles. The audience was impressed by their determination, and the match inspired many spectators to overcome their own hardships.

Finally, in several countries, rugby matches are organized every year to combat bullying at school. These educational encounters highlight the importance of mutual aid and respect, essential values not only in rugby, but also in everyday life. These matches show how sport can have a positive impact far beyond the pitch.

Fact 98 - Games played with futuristic equipment

Rugby, which is constantly evolving, has sometimes been the scene of astonishing experiments with futuristic equipment. These innovations serve not only to improve player performance, but also to make the game safer and more exciting for spectators.

In England, an experimental match was organized using shirts fitted with integrated sensors. These sensors measured speed, impact and even player movement in real time. The data was displayed on screens around the stadium, offering spectators a unique experience.

In New Zealand, special rugby balls fitted with electronic chips were used to record the precise trajectory of the ball. These balls could even signal if a kick had gone over the goalposts or if the ball had gone into touch. This helped referees to make quicker, more accurate decisions.

At a tournament in France, smart mouthguards were introduced. These devices measured the force of impacts sustained by players, alerting coaches to any risk of injury. This innovation was hailed as a major step forward in protecting players while maintaining the intensity of the game.

A friendly match in South Africa tested cleats fitted with micro-sensors to analyze traction on the pitch. This information helped players to adjust their technique according to playing conditions. The experiment showed how technology could be integrated into rugby to improve team performance.

In Australia, spectators were able to use augmented reality glasses during a match. These goggles displayed live statistics, such as the number of passes or tackles made by each player. This transformed the way fans interacted with the game, making every moment even more captivating.

These experimental matches with futuristic equipment do not change the essence of rugby, but show how innovation can enrich the sport. Whether in terms of safety, precision or spectator experience, this equipment adds a new dimension to an already exciting game.

Fact 99 - Teams who played matches at extreme altitudes

Playing rugby at altitude is an extraordinary challenge, where the thin air puts players' physical condition and strategy to the test. Some teams have dared to venture onto pitches perched so high up that even breathing becomes an added difficulty.

One of the most famous matches at altitude took place in La Paz, Bolivia. At an altitude of 3,600 meters, local rugby players took on a team from abroad. The visitors, accustomed to playing at sea level, had to adapt quickly to the oxygen-poor air, making each run far more tiring.

In South Africa, a match was played in Johannesburg, a city already 1,750 meters above sea level. This pitch is regularly used for international matches. The Springboks, accustomed to these conditions, have a clear advantage over unacclimatized opponents, who often suffer from a lack of stamina.

Another impressive example comes from the Andes, where local teams played matches at altitudes of over 4,000 meters. These matches, organized to celebrate the region's sporting culture, attracted the attention of rugby fans from all over the world. The players had to manage not only their breath, but also the intense cold of these heights.

Preparations for these high-altitude matches often include specific training sessions. Teams sometimes travel several days before the match to acclimatize. At these altitudes, strategies change: long runs are limited, and static phases such as scrums become even more crucial.

These extraordinary matches are not just competitions, but also unique opportunities to showcase the spirit of rugby. Whether at the top of the Andes or in the mountains of South Africa, these encounters are a reminder of the resilience of the players and their ability to adapt to extreme environments.

Fact 100 - World rugby's legendary stadiums

Some rugby stadiums are more than just match venues. They tell stories, vibrate with emotion and remain engraved in the memories of players and supporters alike. These arenas have become legendary, hosting unforgettable encounters that have marked the history of the sport.

England's Twickenham Stadium is considered the "home of rugby". With seating for more than 80,000 spectators, it has witnessed a host of English rugby legends and thrilling finals. Fans singing in unison make every match a unique experience.

In New Zealand, Auckland's Eden Park is just as famous. It was here that the All Blacks won their first World Cup in 1987. The atmosphere is electric, and the haka, performed on this pitch, is a thrill for all who attend.

South Africa is home to Ellis Park in Johannesburg, a stadium steeped in history. It was here that the Springboks won the 1995 World Cup, a symbolic event for the entire country. The match was seen as a message of unity in a country marked by apartheid.

The Stade de France in Saint-Denis, near Paris, is the pride and joy of French rugby. Since 1998, it has hosted major matches for Les Bleus. The chants of the fans resonate powerfully under its immense roof, creating an unforgettable atmosphere for international matches.

In Australia, Brisbane's Suncorp Stadium is a must-see venue for the Wallabies. The stadium is renowned for its proximity to the pitch, allowing fans to be close to the action. Matches between Australia and its great rivals are intense and spectacular.

Each of these stadiums is more than just a place to play. They embody the passion for rugby and the memories of the sport's greatest moments. They remind us that rugby is much more than a game: it's a history written on pitches where every meter covered becomes a legend.

Conclusion

Here you are, at the end of this book, and what a journey you've made into the world of rugby! You've discovered amazing facts, incredible players, unforgettable moments and fascinating traditions. This unique sport, with its oval ball and sometimes surprising rules, may have left you wanting to know even more, or even try a pass or tackle yourself. Rugby is an adventure that never ends, and every match is a new story to be written.

By exploring these 100 Facts, you've seen that rugby isn't just about the game, it's also about the spirit. It's about collective strength, where every player counts. It's about respecting your opponent, even in the most intense moments. And it's the desire to surpass oneself, together, to achieve a common goal. These values are just as important off the pitch. Perhaps you've noticed that rugby players and rugbywomen are often great role models in life too.

You've also traveled the world thanks to rugby. From beaches to glaciers, from huge stadiums to small local pitches, this sport is everywhere. It brings together millions of people, whether they play, watch or cheer. While reading these stories, you may have dreamed of one day treading the grass of a mythical stadium, scoring a decisive try, or simply sharing a unique moment with a team.

Rugby is a team story, but it's also your story. Whether you're already an enthusiast or you've simply enjoyed discovering the sport thanks to this book, you're now part of this great oval family. There's still so much to learn, so much to play, so much to experience through rugby, and it all starts with a simple pass or an unpredictable rebound.

So, what will you do now? Maybe you'll put on a jersey, or maybe you'll keep in mind one of the stories you've read here. One thing's for sure: you now know that rugby is a sport where anything is possible. Thank you for sharing this journey, and above all, never forget: whether on or off the pitch, always play with heart, respect and passion.

Marc Dresqui

Quiz

1) What does the scrum-half do during a rugby scrum?

    a)   He pushes forward to gain ground.
    b)   He slips the ball between the two teams to start the action.
    c)   He stays in defence to anticipate a counter-attack.
    d)   He scores points by ducking under the scrum.

2) Why is the rugby ball oval?

    a)   So it's lighter to wear during play.
    b)   Because it's easier to manufacture in this form.
    c)   Because the first bladders used were naturally shaped like this.
    d)   For faster, more precise passing.

3) Why are the British and Irish Lions a unique rugby team?

    a)   Because they only play in Europe.
    b)   Because they are made up of players from the best club teams.
    c)   Because they bring together players from England, Scotland, Wales and Ireland.
    d)   Because they only play local amateur teams.

4) What is the name of the All Blacks' best-known haka?

    a)   Kapa o Pango
    b)   Ka Mate
    c)   Te Rongo
    d)   Haka Tū

5) Which team beat the All Blacks in a series of test matches during the 1971 tour?

    a)   The Springboks
    b)   The Wallabies
    c)   The British and Irish Lions
    d)   The Barbarians

6) What is the main role of the TMO (Télévision Match Officiel) in rugby?

    a)   Communicating with fans in the stands
    b)   Review contentious actions to help make the right decisions
    c)   Signal ball outlets on the sides
    d)   Manage the match timer

7) What was the main objective of the 24-hour rugby match played at Chippenham in 2011?

a) Breaking a game speed record
b) Raise funds for charity
c) Preparing players for an international tournament
d) Testing new game rules

8) What does the delayed whistle mean in a rugby match?

a) Stop play immediately to signal a foul
b) Allow play to continue despite a previous foul
c) Forcing teams to replace players
d) Reducing the time left in a half

9) What philosophy did Graham Henry apply to lead the All Blacks to victory at the 2011 World Cup?

a) Emphasis on raw physical strength
b) Encourage fast, accurate play while taking care of players' mental well-being
c) Introducing technological tools for game analysis
d) Concentrate solely on defensive phases

10) What famous move by Jonny Wilkinson scored the 2003 World Cup Final?

a) A spectacular solo attempt
b) A decisive interception on defense
c) A successful drop goal with just seconds to go
d) A transformation from the sidelines

11) Where did a rugby match take place in 2015, replacing grass with sand?

a) On an aircraft carrier in Australia
b) On a beach in Wales
c) On a glacier in Switzerland
d) In a clearing in New Zealand

12) What is the main aim of a good rugby tackle?

a) Hit the opponent as hard as possible
b) Unbalance the opponent by aiming at the waist or legs
c) Block the opponent by grabbing his neck
d) Use only brute force to stop your opponent

13) Which team ended a run of 36 consecutive defeats in the Six Nations Tournament in 2022?

- a) Scotland
- b) Samoa
- c) Italy
- d) Japan

14) Which rugby player is nicknamed "the fastest man in rugby" thanks to his speed of over 37 km/h?

- a) Bryan Habana
- b) Carlin Isles
- c) Jason Robinson
- d) Jonah Lomu

15) Which player has twice been voted World Rugby Player of the Year thanks to his leadership and outstanding performances?

- a) Pieter-Steph du Toit
- b) Jonah Lomu
- c) Richie McCaw
- d) Dan Carter

16) Which famous player, measuring 1.96 m and weighing 119 kg, is known for his exceptional power and speed on the pitch?

- a) Martin Johnson
- b) Jonah Lomu
- c) Sébastien Vahaamahina
- d) Bakkies Botha

17) Which player was selected for rugby and also excelled in professional boxing?

- a) Jonty Rhodes
- b) Ellyse Perry
- c) Sonny Bill Williams
- d) Jill Burns

18) Which player scored the decisive try for France in the 1987 World Cup semi-final?

- a) Jonah Lomu
- b) Serge Blanco
- c) Jonny Wilkinson
- d) Richie McCaw

19) What can a defensive error cause in a rugby match?

a) An immediate end to the game
b) An opportunity for the opponent to score a try
c) Automatic scrum restart
d) Cancellation of points scored

20) Which stadium is considered the "home of rugby" in England?

a) Eden Park
b) Stade de France
c) Twickenham
d) Ellis Park

Answers

1) What does the scrum-half do during a rugby scrum?

Correct answer: b) He slides the ball between the two teams to start the action.

2) Why is the rugby ball oval?

Correct answer: c) Because the first bladders used were naturally shaped in this way.

3) Why are the British and Irish Lions a unique rugby team?

Correct answer: c) Because they bring together players from England, Scotland, Wales and Ireland.

4) What is the name of the All Blacks' best-known haka?

Correct answer: b) Ka Mate

5) Which team beat the All Blacks in a series of test matches during the 1971 tour?

Correct answer: c) British and Irish Lions

6) What is the main role of the TMO (Télévision Match Officiel) in rugby?

Correct answer: b) Review contentious actions to help make the right decisions

7) What was the main aim of the 24-hour rugby match played at Chippenham in 2011?

Correct answer: b) Raise funds for charities

8) What does the delayed whistle mean in a rugby match?

Correct answer: b) Allow play to continue despite a previous foul

9) What philosophy did Graham Henry apply to lead the All Blacks to victory at the 2011 World Cup?

Correct answer: b) Encourage fast, accurate play while taking care of players' mental well-being

10) What famous move by Jonny Wilkinson scored the 2003 World Cup Final?

Correct answer: c) A successful drop goal with only a few seconds remaining in the match.

11) Where did a rugby match take place in 2015, replacing grass with sand?

Correct answer: b) On a beach in Wales

12) What is the main aim of a good rugby tackle?

Correct answer: b) Unbalance the opponent by aiming at the waist or legs

13) Which team ended a run of 36 consecutive defeats in the Six Nations Tournament in 2022?

Correct answer: c) Italy

14) Which rugby player is nicknamed "the fastest man in rugby" thanks to his speed of over 37 km/h?

Correct answer: b) Carlin Isles

15) Which player has twice been voted World Rugby Player of the Year thanks to his leadership and outstanding performances?

Correct answer: c) Richie McCaw

16) Which famous player, measuring 1.96 m and weighing 119 kg, is known for his exceptional power and speed on the pitch?

Correct answer: b) Jonah Lomu

17) Which player was selected for rugby and also shone in professional boxing?

Correct answer: c) Sonny Bill Williams

18) Which player scored the decisive try for France in the 1987 World Cup semi-final?

Correct answer: b) Serge Blanco

19) What can a defensive error cause in a rugby match?

Correct answer: b) An opportunity for the opponent to score a try

20) Which stadium is considered the "home of rugby" in England?

Correct answer: c) Twickenham

Printed in Great Britain
by Amazon

55365417R00068